"The Mueller investigation was the most important investigation of our lifetime but was also challenging for the public to understand, with charges brought against dozens of individuals and companies. Sara Azari does a great job of cutting through all this detail and making complex legal documents easy to understand."

—**RENATO MARIOTTI**, former federal prosecutor, legal analyst for CNN, and legal affairs columnist for *Politico*

"I'm apolitical. And I investigated for both Special Counsel Robert Fiske and Independent Counsel Ken Starr in the Whitewater investigation of the Clintons. But I could not put this book down. It's engaging, engrossing, and educational. No matter your political leanings, this is a must-read. It lays out and breaks down the legal issues involved in the Russian influence investigation in simple, straightforward language that's easy for everyone to understand. Azari has penned an important work that every U.S. citizen should read."

—**JIM CLEMENTE**, retired FBI supervisory special agent and profiler

"Special Counsel Robert Mueller's investigation was convoluted and daunting to follow, even for lawyers. Sara Azari's experience as a defense attorney and deft hand at explaining the federal criminal world makes her an ideal guide to these historic prosecutions."

—**KEN WHITE**, former federal prosecutor and host of KCRW's *All the President's Lawyers*

"Sara Azari cuts through the political noise to simplify the complexities of the Mueller Report, the main players involved, and what it all means legally. *Unprecedented* serves as an excellent guide for every American to easily understand the extent and impact of the assault on the rule of law and constitutional norms perpetrated by Trump and his associates."

—**TARA SETMAYER**, news political contributor for CNN and ABC, former GOP communications director, board director for Stand Up Republic, and host of *Honestly Speaking with Tara Setmayer* podcast

"Sara Azari's love and passion for the law and this nation are evident throughout the pages of her piece-all-the-facts-together-so-the-people-shall-know book. I applaud her for the courage it took to write it."
—ROLONDA WATTS, journalist, author, actor, podcaster, and talk-show host

"Entertaining, well organized, and well researched, Sara's book will become a historical guide for generations to come. We are indeed living in 'unprecedented' times—which Sara captures perfectly. Never could I have imagined that covering true crime would begin on the steps of the White House. But who would have? A must-read!"
—JOEY JACKSON, legal analyst for CNN and HLN

"*Unprecedented* does an excellent job of documenting the unprecedented and unpresidential crimes of those associated with the Trump administration. Sara Azari explains the crimes, conspiracies, and convictions in a way that is accessible to the general public."
—JOHN HEILMAN, professor at Southwestern Law School

UNPRECEDENTED

UNPREC

★ ★ ★

EDENTED

A SIMPLE GUIDE to the CRIMES of the
TRUMP CAMPAIGN and PRESIDENCY

★ ★ ★

Sara Azari

POTOMAC BOOKS   An imprint of the University of Nebraska Press

Library of Congress Cataloging-in-Publication Data
Names: Azari, Sara, author.
Title: Unprecedented: a simple guide to the crimes of
the Trump campaign and presidency / Sara Azari.
Description: Lincoln: Potomac Books, an imprint of the University
of Nebraska Press, 2020. | Includes bibliographical references.
Identifiers: LCCN 2019034404
ISBN 9781640122994 (hardback)
ISBN 9781640123311 (ebook)
ISBN 9781640123328 (mobi)
ISBN 9781640123335 (pdf)
Subjects: LCSH: Trump, Donald, 1946– | Trump, Donald,
1946– —Friends and associates. | Political corruption—
United States. | Presidents—United States—Election, 2016.
| United States—Politics and government—2017-
Classification: LCC E912 .A93 2020 | DDC 973.933—dc23
LC record available at https://lccn.loc.gov/2019034404

Set in Miller by Laura Ebbeka.
Designed by N. Putens.

CONTENTS

ACKNOWLEDGMENTS

This book is my first, and I appreciate each and every person who has been part of this unprecedented journey.

Even in the simplest form, a book on the crimes of a sitting president and his aides is challenging and owes much to the journalism it follows. I wrote during a stream of breaking news about the criminal violations of the Trump campaign and administration, the president, and the release and ramifications of the Mueller Report. Just as I concluded a chapter and was preparing to move on to the next, I would have to take a detour, circling back to update previous chapters. I owe an immense debt to the journalists who have provided accurate reporting on this topic, especially at the *New York Times*, the *Washington Post*, and CNN.

Many thanks to my family and friends and to my colleagues who encouraged me and believed in the compelling need to write this book. And thank you to my clients who gave me the necessary pause and opportunity to focus on this project. Of course my gratitude also extends to my two pups, Rico and Lola, who were on their best behavior while getting little to no attention, treats, or walks, allowing me to focus on writing.

Also, a very special thanks goes to my editor, Dan Good, and the entire team at Kevin Anderson & Associates. You believed in my project from the beginning and guided me through the crazy publishing process. I'm grateful for all of your hard work and hands-on navigation every step of the way.

Last but not least, my deepest thanks go to my colleagues in the media—anchors and producers—especially my friends at CNN, who have provided me with a platform to decode the law and dispel the noise surrounding the events of the Trump presidency.

I dedicate this book to the memory of my mom and dad, who were spared these unprecedented times. They always believed in me no matter what I strived to do: you are gone, but the ambition, courage, and strength you instilled in me are the foundation for this book.

INTRODUCTION

I am a brown immigrant. I am a lawyer. And I am an American.

As a white-collar criminal defense attorney, I defend individuals accused of crimes in federal district courts nationwide. My path to success has been anything but ordinary or easy. But because of my journey, I have a deeper appreciation for the opportunities, freedom, and protections offered to all Americans under the Constitution and our laws. And I adhere to the basic rule that *no man is above the law, not even the president.*

I chose this career because I have an innate passion for justice and the truth. Up until Donald Trump entered the White House, I considered myself apolitical. But as the investigation into Russian election interference led to criminal indictments against Trump's aides and associates, and as the Mueller Report exposed the president's own obstructive acts, I felt a deep concern that the criminal activity involving President Trump and those in his orbit would set a dangerous precedent for the future of our Constitution, laws, and democracy.

In today's polarized political landscape, many people rely solely on the media for answers. But biased left- and right-leaning media outlets have only added to the noise and confusion of the legal issues surrounding the Trump campaign and presidency, leading to grave misunderstandings. And while the truth is available in convoluted court pleadings and the 448-page Mueller Report, many Americans won't read those documents.

Though I am not a writer by profession, I felt compelled to write this book in an effort to provide an easy reference by which people can better understand the crimes uncovered by the Mueller investigation— criminal acts by a sitting president and key members of his campaign and administration. I also offer potential avenues of justice under federal law for President Trump's obstructive acts and many abuses of power.

Prior to Trump's presidency, a common question I faced was what it meant to represent someone I knew to be guilty, a moral dilemma. I was also regularly asked about true crime cases. Soon after January 20, 2017, the usual cocktail-hour questions shifted to the president's criminality and the crimes and prison terms of his aides and associates. I recognized a palpable need for an accessible handbook that simplifies the crimes of Trumpworld. I endeavor to dispel the myth that the Mueller investigation was a "hoax" and a "witch hunt," as well as to decode the unparalleled abundance of criminal charges under federal law arising from the Mueller probe and spinoff investigations.

The Trump campaign and presidency have most definitely been an exercise in normalizing extraordinary behavior. Sure, we can blame politics for some of the administration's unpresidential acts, lies, and misdeeds. But some things transcend political debate and are indefensible: we cannot excuse or ignore the crimes and constitutional violations committed by President Trump and his campaign. *No man is above the law, not even the president.*

The spectrum of misconduct in the Trump orbit is broad, ranging from ethical violations by cabinet members and White House staffers, crimes committed by numerous campaign and administration officials, to the president's own criminal conduct. Ironically, while the president credited himself with hiring only "the best people," criminal conduct by his cronies showed they were anything but the best. And although some of their violations were unrelated to the president and his campaign, Trump aides and advisors have been convicted of offenses directly connected to the investigation into Russian interference in the 2016 election by Special Counsel Robert S. Mueller III.

Michael Cohen, the president's longtime lawyer and fixer, pleaded guilty to multiple charges including campaign finance law violations for having paid off, in exchange for their silence, two women who claimed they had affairs with Mr. Trump. Paul Manafort and Rick Gates, Trump campaign chairman and deputy campaign chairman, respectively, were also convicted as a result of the Russia probe. Manafort lied to the FBI, a criminal offense under federal law, while Gates pleaded guilty to unrelated financial charges and cooperated in the investigation. Trump campaign foreign policy advisor George Papadopoulos pleaded guilty to lying to the FBI about his contacts with Russians, a common crime in Trumpworld. And Michael Flynn, the president's first national security advisor, also pleaded guilty to lying to the FBI about conversations he had with the Russian ambassador during Donald Trump's presidential transition. Last but not least, Roger Stone, Donald Trump's longtime political advisor, was charged with making false statements, obstruction of proceeding, and witness tampering in connection with the releases of Democrats' emails hacked by Russia. Other than the unrelated financial crimes some of these men committed and Cohen's conviction for campaign finance law violations, the president's aides and associates were all charged with covering up one thing: their contacts, communications, and ties with Russia—the very subject matter of the special counsel's investigation. Yet more stunning than the concerted cover-up of Russian contacts is the revelation of President Trump's own criminal conduct, both as a presidential candidate and while in office. Trump violated campaign finance laws during his candidacy and engaged in brazen instances of obstruction of justice while a sitting president. Those crimes coalesce to form two conclusions: (1) there was a nefarious cover-up related to a foreign adversary's assault on our election in an effort to protect the president, and (2) no president has ever acted in such a self-serving manner as has President Trump, consistently favoring his own interests over the nation's and abusing his powers at every opportunity. The president's criminal conduct and abuse of power have threatened our laws, the Constitution, and democracy.

In nearly two decades, I've defended hundreds of individuals accused of the same criminal activities as the president and his associates. I therefore sympathize with the need for justice and accountability as applied to ALL men, including the president.

When considering President Trump's culpability, it's far too tempting to succumb to political spins and mischaracterizations emanating from the left, the right, the media, politicians, and the White House. Even the president himself has manipulated that noise, weaponizing his tweets to inflame his adversaries and critics, feed his base, misinform the public, and fuel news cycles. The Trump presidency is replete with outrageous lies, cover-ups, and corrupt acts, setting new norms for the highest office of the land. This book does not endeavor to address the entire universe of Trump wrongdoings and violations (I leave that discussion to political experts and analysts). Instead, relying on my knowledge and expertise as a federal practitioner, I provide the reader with a fair and impartial analysis of the criminal and constitutional violations by President Trump and his aides as unveiled by the Mueller investigation.

Interference with the 2016 American election by a foreign adversary, the Trump campaign's dubious contacts with Russians, and the president's criminal acts aimed at obstructing the investigation into the interference as well as his own conduct are detailed and documented in the historic Mueller Report. What follows is my analysis of the crimes committed by key Trump associates as well as a concise outline and interpretation of the Mueller Report's findings, which detail the president's own criminal acts. I provide the reader with a far more genuine and accurate recap of the report than the one released by Attorney General William Barr, whose four-page biased and mischaracterized "summary" was written for one reason: to falsely exonerate his boss.

In closing, I leave you with the necessary consequences of the president's abuse of power and criminal conduct: the impeachment, removal, and indictment of President Donald J. Trump. *No man is above the law, not even the president.*

UNPRECEDENTED

CHAPTER 1

GEORGE D. PAPADOPOULOS

THE LOOSE-LIPPED "COFFEE BOY"

★ ★ ★ ★ ★

Association: Foreign policy advisor to the 2016 Donald Trump campaign

Crime: One count of violating Title 18 U.S.C. § 1001 (making false statements)

Sentence: Fourteen days (actually served twelve days)

Somebody had to take the first fall in Robert Mueller's investigation, and that honor goes to a former Trump campaign foreign policy advisor, George Papadopoulos. Although he may be the smallest fish in terms of the severity of his crime and his proximity to then-candidate Trump compared with other indicted men in the investigation, his case—the first to be fully adjudicated—paved the road to the unprecedented crimes of Trumpworld. This case and what follows go beyond issues of political differences about wrongdoing and disputes about facts and alternative facts. The case of George Papadopoulos marks the beginning of this book's travels down the road of indictable criminal activity by those close to the president and his campaign. Each chapter that follows further unravels the tangled web of lies (a recurring theme in this book) and crimes of the top senior officials and aides implicated during the election, the transition, and the Trump presidency.

Papadopoulos was arrested on July 27, 2017, and charged with lying to the FBI about his efforts and conversations with Russian officials to broker a relationship between Trump and Vladimir Putin. Trump, the White House staff, and former campaign officials have downplayed

Papadopoulos's importance to distance themselves from his crime. But twenty-nine-year-old Papadopoulos was apparently a key to questions about the campaign's contacts with Russian officials, particularly related to the hacking incident that led to the WikiLeaks release of Hillary Clinton's controversial emails from her private server when she was secretary of state. Papadopoulos pleaded guilty to the charges on October 5, 2017, cementing his place in history as the first person to be convicted and serve prison time in the special counsel's investigation of the Trump campaign. Clearly, this isn't exactly how Papadopoulos wanted history to remember him.

George Demetrios Papadopoulos grew up around politics. He was born in Chicago in 1987 to Greek immigrants, and his father, a physician, was politically active in Chicago's Greek American community. This environment spurred George to study political science at DePaul University, where he became deeply involved in Greek, Turkish, and Cypriot politics. After graduating with a bachelor's degree, he completed his master's degree at the University College London's School of Public Policy. Intent on making his mark in politics, he took an unpaid internship at the conservative Hudson Institute, a think tank known for foreign policy work, and then left four years later for a London-based position with the oil and gas advisory firm Energy Stream.

Papadopoulos was and still is something of a mystery man. Few people who know him well, including his neighbors in Lincolnwood, Illinois, have talked with reporters. Professors at DePaul don't remember him, one having stated that Papadopoulos didn't perform well enough in class to be known. But multiple accounts from people who worked with him or knew him casually from the same social circles paint a portrait of a man who is a legend in his own mind and obsessed with becoming a political mover and shaker. Confident, brash, ambitious, conceited, puffed up, "vain to a fault"—these are a few of their choice words to describe Papadopoulos, traits that ultimately led to his downfall.

Breaking into National Politics

A series of coordinated terrorist attacks in Paris on November 13, 2015, sent U.S. presidential candidates scurrying to find foreign policy experts for their campaigns, but few were available at the time, and the top names were already committed to frontrunners Jeb Bush and Marco Rubio. This problem led Barry Bennett, the campaign manager for candidate Ben Carson, to focus on the résumé of an unknown energy consultant whose studies abroad and focus on security seemed to fit the campaign's needs. But what stood out most on Papadopoulos's résumé were his years at the Hudson Institute (note: he was an unpaid intern, though the résumé implied he was an employee). When Bennett called his friend Kenneth Weinstein (Hudson's president) for a reference, Weinstein told him that he hardly knew Papadopoulos, but added, "He's junior, he's smart." That, along with Papadopoulos's promise to raise campaign donations from the Greek American community, was enough for Bennett, who was desperate to fill the position.

Later, when Carson dropped out of the presidential race, Papadopoulos moved back to Chicago and applied for a position with Trump's campaign. Despite his mediocre political career, he was hired in early March 2016 as one of five foreign policy advisors. This was an interesting turn that puzzled many observers in political circles because this was the first time they had ever heard of Papadopoulos, and they questioned his credentials. Meanwhile, in an interview with the *Washington Post* editorial board, Trump described him to journalists as an "excellent guy." Foreign policy advisor to a presidential candidate's campaign is a heady title, and Papadopoulos set out to prove himself worthy of it.

Involvement with the Trump Campaign

In his job interview with then Trump campaign aide Sam Clovis, Papadopoulos was told that one of Trump's priorities would be improving the relationship between Russia and the United States, a statement Clovis has denied. Papadopoulos now had a goal and needed a chance to prove himself in this regard to the Trump orbit. Only days after joining the campaign, while attending a conference in Rome for the London Centre, Papadopoulos met Joseph Mifsud, a professor from Malta who was affiliated with the London Centre. Mifsud showed little interest in Papadopoulos until he learned of his position with the Trump campaign. Then the professor started bragging about his connections to the Russian government and the Russian Foreign Ministry, and he suggested that he and Papadopoulos had a common interest in arranging for Trump to meet with Russian officials, particularly Vladimir Putin. Mifsud hastily set up a meeting in London between Papadopoulos and Olga Polonskaya, a woman he said was Putin's niece (this turned out to be a lie). He also introduced Papadopoulos to Ivan Timofeev of the prestigious Valdai Discussion Club, a group of scholars that meets with Putin yearly. Papadopoulos and Timofeev communicated for months about connecting the Trump campaign with Russian officials.

After meeting with Olga Polonskaya on March 24, 2016, Papadopoulos sent an email to Trump campaign officials with the subject line: "Meeting with Russian Leadership—Including Putin," offering to set up a meeting "between us and the Russian leadership." Papadopoulos claimed that his Russian contacts were eager for such a meeting, in which relations between the two countries would be discussed. Trump's top advisors were stunned and had several concerns. They feared that such a meeting might violate U.S. sanctions against Russia and the Logan Act (a law enacted in 1799 that makes it a crime for unauthorized persons to negotiate with foreign governments that have a dispute with the United States) and thought that no plans should be made without consulting with NATO allies first. But Papadopoulos persisted and for months continued sending email requests for a meeting. In mid-April, Polonskaya emailed Papadopoulos to say, "We are all very excited by the possibility of a good relationship with Mr. Trump."

Papadopoulos also continued communicating with Mifsud, who in late April told him that the Russians had politically damaging "dirt" on candidate Hillary Clinton in the form of "thousands of emails" that Russian hackers mined from her private email server. Papadopoulos emailed Stephen Miller, then a senior policy advisor to the Trump campaign, saying that he had "interesting messages coming in from Moscow." A couple of weeks later, Papadopoulos's penchant for puffery was the spark that lit a raging fire.

In early May while having drinks in London with Australian diplomat Alexander Downer, Papadopoulos openly bragged that Russia had political dirt on Hillary Clinton from thousands of hacked Democratic National Committee (DNC) emails the Russians had stolen apparently to damage her campaign. Two months later, the emails started appearing online, which spurred Australian officials to finally tell their U.S. counterparts about Downer's encounter with Papadopoulos. These two factors prompted the FBI to open a counterintelligence investigation into Russian election interference and the possibility that candidate Trump's associates were conspiring with Russia to steal the election.

The Investigation

The FBI quietly opened an investigation that senior agents didn't discuss even in classified settings. Besides the information from the Australians, the FBI received intelligence from the British and Dutch governments, taking note of others making connections with Russia, including Trump campaign advisor Carter Page. Keeping the investigation on the sly, the FBI waited more than eight months before finally interviewing Papadopoulos in late January 2017, several days after Donald Trump's inauguration. As Papadopoulos attended the lavish parties and rubbed elbows with senior transition officials, looking forward to the new year filled with possibilities for his political career, his worst nightmare was about to unfold.

The FBI interviewed Papadopoulos twice—on January 27 and February 16. After the February meeting, Papadopoulos deleted all of his social media accounts, and what he was doing between February and October of that year is largely unreported. What happened in the next two months, however, changed his life.

On May 17 the Department of Justice named Robert S. Mueller

III, a well-regarded veteran FBI director, as special counsel to take over the investigation of Russian meddling in the 2016 presidential election and possible collusion between Russian agents and Trump associates.

On October 30, 2017, Mueller dropped a bombshell by unsealing documents revealing that Papadopoulos had been arrested on July 27, charged with lying to the FBI in his interviews earlier in the year (a violation of Title 18 United States Code Section 1001, abbreviated as Title 18 U.S.C. § 1001). According to the unsealed plea agreement, Papadopoulos had pleaded guilty in early October and had been cooperating with the investigation to avoid further prosecution.

Papadopoulos's guilty plea resulted from lying to the FBI about the timing and significance of his many conversations with people he thought were close to the Russian government. That it was the first fall in the Mueller investigation was news enough, but the fact that Papadopoulos had been cooperating with the special counsel's team since his arrest was the real shocker. The Trump White House and former campaign officials responded with denial and damage control efforts, trying to lessen Papadopoulos's importance with schoolboy name-calling. Former campaign manager Corey Lewandowski called Papadopoulos a "low-level volunteer," a term echoed by President Trump, who tweeted: "Few people knew the young, low-level volunteer named George, who has already proven to be a liar." Former Trump campaign advisor Michael Caputo said, "The guy was—he was the coffee boy." Press Secretary Sarah Huckabee Sanders insisted that Papadopoulos had an "extremely limited" role in the campaign in his "volunteer position," and stated, "His guilty plea has nothing to do with his campaign activities—only his failure to be honest about them." Even Barry Bennett piled on, saying Papadopoulos "was someone who worked for me at the Carson campaign for, like, fifteen minutes."

Only a fool would call Papadopoulos a "low-level volunteer" or a "coffee boy." Campaigns routinely employ volunteers at all levels, including the most experienced advisors. A prime spot on the Trump campaign's foreign policy team is hardly a low-level position, so Papadopoulos's volunteer status doesn't diminish his role or importance. In fact, in a meeting with the *Washington Post* editorial board, Trump called him "an excellent guy," a complete contradiction. The unsealing of Papadopoulos's plea agreement (coupled with the same-day announcement of Paul Manafort's indictment) was a prelude to additional targets and future charges in the Mueller investigation.

Crime and Cooperation

There's a recurring theme of lying that follows this chapter. We learn early in life that lying is wrong. Though prevalent in politics, lying is immoral to some and even sinful to others. However, lying isn't always a crime. This book addresses those lies that *are* a crime and subject to penalty and punishment under the law.

Upon his arrest, Papadopoulos began cooperating with the Mueller team, providing them with valuable information. Cooperators are required to provide full and candid information to federal authorities. Sometimes they're also wired so that communications with targets can be recorded as evidence against them. There's no room for half-truths, omissions, or lies when someone agrees to cooperate with federal prosecutors and agents. Successful cooperation leads to a reduced sentence for the cooperator and, in some limited instances, an agreement by the government not to prosecute the individual. When a defendant cooperates fully and truthfully, prosecutors file what's known as a 5K1.1 motion (often referred to as a letter) informing the court of the level and quality of the defendant's cooperation and a recommendation for a reduced sentence.

Papadopoulos's plea agreement was sealed. Plea agreements are typically sealed in ongoing investigations because the agreement contains details of the defendant's cooperation. If a cooperation plea agreement were to be publicly accessible, it would not only potentially tip off other targets under investigation but also interfere with the ongoing investigation. It's also important to the investigation to keep any cooperator's identity as covert as possible for their safety and so they're not targeted or ostracized.

In Papadopoulos's case, his arrest was based on suspicion of illicit contact with Russian officials during the Trump campaign. Although he agreed to cooperate, he lied to federal agents in his two interviews on January 27 and February 16, 2017. Those lies led to the offense conduct to which he pleaded: a violation of Title 18 U.S.C. § 1001, commonly known as *making false statements*.

On October 5, 2017, Papadopoulos pleaded guilty to one count of making false statements. To be found guilty of this offense, the defendant must admit the following:

1. He made a false statement in a matter within the jurisdiction of a specific branch of government (in Papadopoulos's case, the Department of Justice, namely the FBI);
2. He acted willfully (meaning deliberately and with knowledge that his statements were not true); and
3. The statements were material to the agency's decisions or activities.

Papadopoulos pleaded guilty because he deliberately lied about several material facts within his knowledge:

a. He interacted with Mifsud *before* being named as a foreign policy advisor to the Trump campaign, and thus he wasn't with the campaign when Mifsud told him about having "thousands of emails" that would be damaging to then-candidate Hillary Clinton. *Contrary to his misrepresentation*, Papadopoulos learned that he would be a campaign advisor in early March 2016; Mifsud met with Papadopoulos on or about March 14, *only* because Papadopoulos was a campaign advisor; and Mifsud told Papadopoulos about the emails on or about April 26, at a time when Papadopoulos had been a campaign advisor for more than a month.

b. Mifsud was "a nothing" and "just a guy talk[ing] up connections or something." *Contrary to this misrepresentation*, the evidence supported Papadopoulos's belief that Mifsud had substantial connections to Russian government officials and had met with some of them in Moscow right before telling him about the damaging emails, and Papadopoulos sought to use these connections for several months in order to arrange a meeting between the Trump campaign and Russian government officials.

c. He met the female Russian national *before* he joined the Trump campaign and their communications were limited to generic email exchanges that said, "Hi, how are you?" *Contrary to this misrepresentation*, the investigation revealed that Papadopoulos had in fact met the female Russian national on or about March 24, 2016, *after* he became a campaign advisor; that he believed that she had connections to Russian government officials; and that he sought to use her Russian connections for several months to arrange a meeting between the Trump campaign and Russian government officials.

Sentence

The maximum sentence for a violation of Title 18 U.S.C. § 1001 is five years in prison. However, without a mandatory minimum sentence under a given statute, the sentence for felonies and serious misdemeanors under federal law is determined by applying the U.S. Federal Sentencing Guidelines, a set of rules developed as a result of the Sentencing Reform Act of 1984. The guidelines are designed to avoid sentencing disparities. Under the guidelines, the applicable sentencing range for a violation of Title 18 U.S.C. § 1001 by someone who, like Papadopoulos, was a first-time offender with no criminal history, is zero to six months.

Because Papadopoulos was the first to be sentenced in the investigation, his attorneys feared that prosecutors would try to use him as an example to send a strong message to those who followed. In their sentencing papers, they sought leniency arguing that Papadopoulos's

lies had no impact on the Mueller investigation. But Title 18 U.S.C. §
1001 doesn't carve out exceptions for the size of the lie: no matter how
big or small the lie, any statement that is a "materially false, fictitious,
or fraudulent statement or representation" violates this law. Papadopoulos's sentence is perhaps the most interesting aspect of his case.

On September 7, 2018, Papadopoulos was sentenced to two weeks
in prison. The sentence is lawful and fits the crime, but in practicality,
most first-time offenders who are cooperating with authorities would
qualify for probation and avoid a prison sentence altogether. Papadopoulos was a first-time offender with no criminal history and no
aggravating circumstances. But in a high-profile case with a backdrop
of politics involving national security, our elections, democracy, and the
president of the United States, Papadopoulos's sentence was clearly a
loud message to those following him in the investigation: you better
not lie when you're speaking to government agents and prosecutors!

According to Mueller's sentencing memo, which sought a prison sentence for Papadopoulos, "The defendant's crime was serious and caused
damage to the government's investigation into Russian interference in
the 2016 presidential election." The memo highlights that Papadopoulos
was explicitly informed of the seriousness of the investigation and was
warned that lying to investigators was a "federal offense" that could get
him "in trouble." It also states that Papadopoulos's lies were "not only
deliberate, but repeated." The document details Papadopoulos's conduct
during the interviews and concludes that the facts and circumstances
warrant incarceration.

On November 26, 2018, Papadopoulos surrendered to the Federal
Correctional Institution in Oxford, Wisconsin, and began serving his
sentence. He was released on December 7 after serving only twelve
days of the fourteen-day sentence. The shortage of two days is based on
applicable custody credits. In addition to incarceration, Papadopoulos's
sentence includes payment of a $9,500 fine, twelve months of supervised
release, and completion of two hundred hours of community service.

Immediately after his release, Papadopoulos announced his first speaking engagement, a forthcoming book, *Deep State Target: How I Got Caught in the Crosshairs of the Plot to Bring Down President Trump*, and his 2020 campaign for a congressional seat. We don't know what will come of Papadopoulos's political aspirations, but we do know that even a "low-level coffee boy" can be convicted of a felony and sentenced to time in prison. Clearly, George Papadopoulos, despite his beliefs to the contrary, is not above the law. The following chapters will demonstrate that the law is the law, and nobody—regardless of rank, title, involvement, and proximity to the president or his campaign—is above the law

CHAPTER 2

LT. GEN. (RET.) MICHAEL FLYNN

THE GENERAL WHO KNEW BETTER

★ ★ ★ ★ ★

Association: National security advisor

Crime: One count of violating Title 18 U.S.C. § 1001 (making false statements)

Sentence: TBD

"Lock her up," Lt. Gen. (Ret.) Michael Flynn said from the floor of the Republican National Convention on July 18, 2016, repeating the crowd's chanting against Democratic candidate Hillary Clinton. It was an odd moment for one of the most highly respected and heavily decorated members of the U.S. military—someone who had years before led the Defense Intelligence Agency, the Pentagon's intelligence arm, under President Barack Obama. Ironically, less than eighteen months later, it was Flynn, not Clinton, who would face charges for making false statements to the FBI about his communication with Russia. Flynn's arrest marked the most jarring of Robert Mueller's investigation because of how respected he was and how far he had fallen. Where others arguably may not have recognized the letter of the law, Flynn knew better.

Flynn had already been under FBI scrutiny when he joined President Trump's transition team and became his national security advisor. With a few phone calls to Russia and the lies that followed, Flynn created a firestorm for the Trump administration, destroyed the reputation he had spent decades cultivating, and helped set the wheels in motion for the firing of FBI director James Comey—a personnel move that contributed to the appointment of Special Counsel Robert Mueller.

Michael Thomas Flynn was born to a large Irish Catholic family in Rhode Island on December 24, 1958. Flynn's parents embodied the focuses he would embrace in adulthood. His father was a career army noncommissioned officer, while his mother was involved in politics and graduated from law school at age sixty-three. He spent his childhood surfing, playing sports, and cliff-diving—a good kid with a rebellious streak.

Flynn went on to graduate from the ROTC program at the University of Rhode Island before joining the army. He wound up serving in combat zones for five years—in Grenada, Haiti, Iraq, and Afghanistan. His intelligence aided in his rise through the ranks, and his wit and cavalier attitude made him a free-thinking leader. Flynn served sixteen years as a paratrooper and qualified as an elite U.S. Army Ranger with more than 150 combat training jumps to his credit. He also served as the senior intelligence officer for the Eighty-Second Airborne Division and for the Eighteenth Airborne Corps. In 2002, he was named director of intelligence for U.S. forces in Afghanistan. He also served as director of intelligence for the Joint Special Operations Command, director of intelligence for the U.S. Central Command, director of intelligence for the Joint Chiefs of Staff, assistant director of national intelligence in the Office of the Director of National Intelligence, and finally, director of the Defense Intelligence Agency. But in his role with DIA Flynn ruffled feathers with his outspokenness and clashed with members of President Obama's administration, frustrated by his view that the administration wasn't doing enough to curb the spread of ISIS and other terrorist groups in the Middle East. And in 2014, he was nudged to take an early retirement and pushed to the sidelines.

National Politics

While Flynn was apolitical throughout much of his career, his outspokenness about Obama's administration grew louder after he departed as DIA director. He began appearing on Fox News, and later RT, Russian state television. In December 2015, RT paid more than $45,000 for

Flynn to appear at a gala in Moscow honoring RT—Flynn received more than $33,000 of that total. At the function, he was photographed sitting next to Russian president Vladimir Putin, a moment that concerned U.S. intelligence agents who feared Flynn was being manipulated by the Kremlin.

As the 2016 election cycle picked up steam, Flynn began offering foreign policy advice to Republican presidential candidates. But one candidate stood above the rest, New York real estate developer Donald Trump. On the surface, Trump and Flynn had little in common. Trump, entitled and egotistical, had avoided serving in Vietnam under the ruse of having developed "bone spurs" and insulted Gold Star families, relatives of troops who had died. Flynn, with his working-class roots, had spent his adult life serving his country and knew far too well the sacrifices of military duty. But they found common ground in their disdain for Obama and frustration in the belief that political correctness had run amok. So after Trump emerged as the Republican presidential favorite, Flynn became one of Trump's most outspoken supporters.

Involvement with the Trump Campaign

Trump was so enamored of Flynn that he almost made the retired general his running mate, even though Flynn was a registered Democrat and was vocal about abortion rights. In the end, Trump chose Indiana governor Mike Pence. Nonetheless, Flynn had a key mission that summer—find Hillary Clinton's missing emails. His "lock her up" speech at the RNC wasn't just empty talk. During the summer of 2016, after Trump began calling for Clinton's emails, Flynn "contacted multiple people in an effort to obtain" the lost messages, Robert Mueller wrote in his report. Two of the people Flynn contacted were investment advisor Peter Smith and Barbara Ledeen, a GOP Senate staffer whose husband had written a book with Flynn.

On August 17, Flynn attended Trump's first intelligence briefing—a briefing in which Russia and other foreign adversaries were highlighted. He also shared content on Twitter that was generated by Russian operatives.

Flynn's conduct had been concerning enough that his former boss decided to speak up about it. On November 10, when Obama met Trump in the Oval Office, Obama warned his successor about Flynn, saying he wasn't the right fit for a lofty position in Trump's administration, and days later, a report emerged alleging that Flynn's consulting firm was lobbying for Turkish interests. Flynn's connections to Russia and Turkey had most definitely drawn FBI scrutiny. But the red flags and warnings didn't deter Trump, who named Flynn his national security advisor just one week later.

Flynn's questionable overseas connections continued during his work on Trump's transition team. Weeks after Election Day, Flynn and Jared Kushner, Donald Trump's son-in-law and a senior transition team member, met Russian ambassador Sergey Kislyak at Trump Tower to discuss the possibility of setting up a back channel between the Kremlin and the Trump team. On December 22, 2016, at Kushner's urging, Flynn also made calls hoping to influence a United Nations Security Council resolution involving Israeli settlements. The resolution was brought by Egypt, and Flynn called government officials in several countries, including Russia, about their stance on the resolution. The resolution would be approved by a 14–0 vote, with the United States abstaining.

Flynn's Russia connections drew renewed scrutiny after Obama announced sanctions on December 29 for the country's attempts to meddle in the U.S. presidential election. But instead of a tit-for-tat retaliation, Putin remained calm, saying he was "reserving the right to retaliate" but optimistic to work with the incoming administration. Hours later, President-elect Trump responded to Putin's statement on Twitter: "Great move on delay (by V. Putin)."

As it turns out, Flynn had spoken on the phone with Sergey Kislyak after the sanctions had been announced, urging Russia to refrain from escalating the situation in order to maintain a good relationship with the incoming administration. In a second phone call, Kislyak confirmed Russia wouldn't retaliate. News of the phone calls started coming into focus when the *Washington Post* reported on them on January 12, 2017. At that time, days before Trump's inauguration, Flynn denied to senior administration officials, including Vice President-elect Mike Pence, that he had discussed sanctions with Kislyak. But based on its surveillance of Flynn, the FBI knew the story Flynn told Pence was false. Pence and Press Secretary Sean Spicer both publicly repeated Flynn's false account.

The FBI asked Flynn for an interview, and he agreed. Without his lawyers present, Flynn met with FBI agents on January 24. He was among the first Trump aides to meet with the FBI regarding the counterintelligence investigation into Russia's interference. Flynn was "relaxed and jocular," and he offered to give a tour of the area around his West Wing office, the agents recalled. He was not warned about the penalties for making false statements to the FBI, given that, due to his long military career, he would be well aware that lying to the FBI was a crime. Regardless, he continued to lie, telling agents he had not discussed sanctions with Kislyak. He also made false statements to the FBI about his contacts with Russia concerning the UN resolution about Israeli settlements in December 2016.

In late January 2017, Acting Attorney General Sally Yates contacted White House counsel Donald McGahn. McGahn then passed those concerns to Trump, who was extremely concerned about the scandal enveloping Flynn. On January 27, the seventh full day of his presidency, Trump invited FBI director James Comey to a private dinner at the White House and sought loyalty from Comey. According to notes taken by Comey, Trump also claimed that Flynn had "serious judgment issues." The scandal intensified, and in mid-February Trump requested Flynn's resignation. As Flynn was set to depart, they hugged. "We'll give you a good recommendation. You're a good guy. We'll take care of you," Trump said to him. Sean Spicer told the media that Flynn resigned not because of a legal issue "but based on a trust issue, a level of trust between the president and General Flynn had eroded to the point where [Trump] felt he had to make a change." Trump, of course, blamed the media. "General Flynn is a wonderful man. I think he's been treated very, very unfairly by the media," Trump told reporters on February 15. Following Flynn's removal, Trump had another meeting with Comey in the Oval Office. "I hope you can see your way clear to letting this go, to letting Flynn go. He is a good guy. I hope you can let this go," Trump told Comey, according to Comey's notes. But Comey and the DOJ refused to comply. On May 9 Trump fired Comey, later blaming the decision on the Russia investigation, among other pretexts.

Comey's termination put Attorney General Jeff Sessions in an awkward position. Sessions had been the chair of the Trump campaign's National Security Advisory Committee, and he was present at a March 31, 2016, meeting at which foreign policy advisor George Papadopoulos suggested he could arrange a meeting between Trump and Putin. Sessions had also had at least one formal meeting and multiple encounters with Ambassador Kislyak in 2016. Given the conflict of interest, Sessions recused himself from the Russia investigation, handing the duties to Deputy Attorney General Dana Boente, clearing the way for the special counsel, Robert Mueller, to be appointed.

Trump continued holding Flynn in high regard, painting the former national security advisor as a victim. According to the Mueller Report, White House insiders believe the president's support of Flynn following the firing was motivated by his desire "to keep Flynn from saying negative things about him." It was "good vibes only" for months, and Flynn and Trump entered a joint defense agreement that allowed their lawyers to share information. But by November 2017 Flynn's legal team had stopped sharing information with Trump's lawyers, and in December it was revealed that Flynn had been cooperating with the government. When Flynn withdrew from the joint defense agreement, the president's personal counsel left a message for Flynn's attorneys "reminding them of the President's warm feelings towards Flynn, which he said 'still remains,' and asking for a 'heads up' if Flynn knew 'information that implicates the President.'" Upon reiteration by Flynn's attorneys that he could no longer share information with Team Trump, Trump's counsel responded he would make sure to pass along Flynn's "hostility" toward the president.

Despite the disgraceful nature of Flynn's conduct, the Mueller team highlighted Flynn's long, storied career and service in its December 2018 sentencing memorandum. "The defendant's record of military and public service distinguish him from every other person who has been charged as part of the SCO's investigation," Mueller wrote. "However, senior government leaders should be held to the highest standards. The defendant's extensive government service should have made him particularly aware of the harm caused by providing false information to the government, as well as the rules governing work performed on behalf of a foreign government." U.S. District Court Judge Emmet Sullivan clearly adopted this sentiment to the 1,000th degree, asking during a December court hearing whether Flynn's behavior "rises to the level of treasonous activity."

Crime and Cooperation

On December 1, 2017, Flynn pleaded guilty to making false statements to FBI agents, a violation of Title 18 U.S.C. § 1001. As a factual basis supporting the offense, Mueller cited Flynn's lies about his phone calls with Ambassador Kislyak in December 2016 as well as his misleading Foreign Agents Registration Act (FARA) filing in March 2017 in which Flynn omitted details about his business relationship with the Republic of Turkey. Following his guilty plea, Flynn expressed remorse. "It has been extraordinarily painful to endure these many months of false accusations of 'treason' and other outrageous acts," Flynn said in a statement. "The actions I acknowledged in court today were wrong, and, through my faith in God, I am working to set things right. My guilty plea and agreement to cooperate with the Special Counsel's

Office reflect a decision I made in the best interests of my family and of our country."

Some legal experts believed Flynn's interactions with Russia violated the Logan Act, a 1799 law forbidding negotiations by unauthorized persons with foreign governments having a dispute with the United States, but he was spared that charge, and in fact, no one has ever been successfully prosecuted for a Logan Act violation.

As discussed earlier, to be found guilty of a violation of 18 USC § 1001, the defendant must admit the following:

1. He made a false statement in a matter within the jurisdiction of a specific branch of government (in Flynn's case, the Department of Justice, namely the FBI).
2. He acted willfully (meaning deliberately and with knowledge that his statements were not true).
3. The statements were material to the agency's decisions or activities.

Flynn pleaded guilty to this offense because he willfully lied to FBI agents about material facts within his knowledge, namely, that:

a. At the January 24, 2017, meeting with FBI agents when Flynn was interviewed regarding the investigation into Russia's interference with the 2016 election, while knowing his statements were not true, he vehemently denied discussing sanctions with Kislyak.
b. Also at the January 24 meeting, Flynn made false statements about his contacts with Russia concerning the December 2016 UN resolution. He stated that he did not request any countries to take a particular action on the resolution, only asking their position on the vote. He also lied to the agents by stating that Russia's ambassador never described Russia's response about the resolution. All of this Flynn knew to be false.

Flynn's lies were in fact "material," as they went to the heart of the investigation: whether or not there were contacts and coordination between members of the Trump orbit and Russian officials.

Sentence

By the time of his December 18, 2018, sentencing hearing, Flynn had sat down for nineteen interviews with the Special Counsel's Office and other DOJ attorneys, cooperating with several ongoing investigations. According to a December addendum to the Mueller team's sentencing memorandum, Flynn had also provided documents and communications to assist with the investigation. Mueller cited Flynn's cooperation with the SCO investigation as a reason why others were more forthcoming with investigators. Ahead of the December sentencing hearing, the Special Counsel's Office team asked Judge Sullivan to consider sentencing Flynn to a term at the low end of the guidelines of zero to six months due to Flynn's "substantial assistance to the government, and that the offense level and guideline range do not account for a downward departure pursuant to Section 5K1.1" of the U.S. Federal Sentencing Guidelines.

Flynn's legal team pleaded for a sentence of probation and community service, a term below the applicable guidelines, citing his "genuine contrition for the uncharacteristic error in judgment," as well as his "deep respect" for the law. Judge Sullivan nixed the suggestions by the prosecutors and defense, instead asking Mueller if he had considered charging Flynn with "treason" and telling Flynn "arguably you sold your country out." Instead of sentencing Flynn, Sullivan urged Flynn to agree to a delay in order to continue cooperating. By early 2019, other than potentially testifying at a future trial, Flynn's cooperation with the government had been completed, clearing the way for his sentencing.

Flynn's December sentencing hearing is a reminder that at sentencing, a federal judge is not bound by the agreements between a defendant and the government. The judge has the broad discretion to issue a sentence that is legal and outside of the range agreed to. This is so despite a defendant's extensive cooperation. In spite of Flynn's honorable decades of service to the country, the mitigating individual characteristics under Title 18 U.S.C. § 3553, his lack of criminal history, the prosecution's praise in the 5K1.1 motion to the court regarding his cooperation, and the Mueller team's suggestion that Flynn be sentenced to the low end of the guidelines—which could mean probation—Judge Sullivan was unwilling to adopt a sentence consistent with the parties' positions and the facts and circumstances of Flynn's cooperation and record before the court. Sullivan instead said in more ways than one that because of Flynn's history as a decorated military officer who was director of the Defense Intelligence Agency, he should be held to a higher standard. Sullivan indicated that if the sentencing moved forward on December 18, the term would have been far greater than the one Flynn was seeking. Sullivan suggested that he would be willing to consider additional cooperation by Flynn, if any, at a future sentencing date. In other words, given everything before Sullivan on December 18, 2018, he disagreed with a sentence at the low end of the guidelines and certainly probation, and he required additional information to reconsider such a sentence at a later time.

In May 2019, it was reported that while awaiting sentencing, Flynn had engaged in a pattern of modulation, oscillating between providing substantial assistance to the Mueller team and undermining the investigation. In April 2018, after having entered into a cooperation plea agreement with the Mueller team, Flynn sent a Twitter direct message to Representative Matt Gaetz, a Florida Republican, encouraging him to "keep the pressure on" after Gaetz was on Fox News ripping the investigation. "You stay on top of what you're doing. Your leadership is so vital for our country right now." Flynn also sent Gaetz GIFs of a bald eagle and American flag on February 14, 2019, the day Attorney General William Barr was confirmed. While the substance of the communications alone may not violate the law or be deemed a breach of Flynn's plea agreement, it does demonstrate poor cooperation etiquette. Flynn was playing on both teams, providing substantial assistance in the Mueller investigation while separately and simultaneously encouraging one of the investigation's most vocal critics to continue publicly undermining Mueller's efforts. It's unclear if the special counsel learned of the messages prior to the December sentencing hearing, when prosecutors recommended little to no prison time for Flynn. Regardless, the communications don't help Flynn's cause. Instead they support Judge Sullivan's impression of Flynn: that he lacked contrition and "deep respect" for the law. Flynn's unilateral communications with Gaetz may certainly further impact his chances at the probationary sentence his lawyers are seeking.

Despite the scandal that surrounded Flynn, there's strong speculation that the president could consider pardoning his former national security advisor. After all, he has continuously viewed the Russia investigation as a scam—repeatedly calling it a "hoax," "witch hunt," and "illegal"—and is reportedly sympathetic to the personal and financial toll Flynn has endured (his legal fees are estimated to top $5 million). In June 2019, pending a continued sentencing hearing, Flynn surprisingly retained new counsel, former federal prosecutor Sidney Powell, a conspiracy theorist who previously suggested Flynn should withdraw his guilty plea in the case. "Extraordinary manipulation by powerful people led to the creation of Robert Mueller's continuing investigation and prosecution of General Michael Flynn," she wrote in a 2018 *Daily Caller* op-ed. Although defendants have the right to be represented by counsel of their choice at any stage of the proceedings against them, Flynn's selection of Powell and the timing of his substitution of attorney raises a red flag: Is this all a precursor to Flynn withdrawing his guilty plea? Or a means of pleasing President Trump toward continued praise and a pardon? Pardon or no pardon, Flynn's crime was no hoax, and it turned a three-star general into a convicted felon.

CHAPTER 3

RICK GATES

THE DISLOYAL ASSOCIATE

★ ★ ★ ★ ★

Association: Deputy manager, 2016 Donald Trump campaign

Crime: One count of violating Title 18 U.S.C. § 371 (conspiracy against the United States), and one count of violating Title 18 U.S.C. § 1001 (making false statements)

Sentence: TBD

Not all of the misconduct uncovered in Special Counsel Robert Mueller's investigation relates directly to Donald Trump's campaign. Some aides, such as deputy campaign manager Rick Gates, were ensnared due to crimes carried out years prior to entering Trump's orbit. But the case of Rick Gates, much like that of his longtime mentor Paul Manafort, speaks to a recurring theme of the president surrounding himself with dishonest people and highlights a moral decay that permeated the campaign. Along with the efforts to obtain dirt on Democratic challenger Hillary Clinton by any means necessary, that moral decay intensified after Manafort and Gates joined the campaign. While Rick Gates was one of the first Trump campaign officials to face charges in the investigation—the indictments of Manafort and Gates were announced on October 30, 2017, the same day foreign policy advisor George Papadopoulos's guilty plea was revealed—his sentencing was delayed for more than a year due to his ongoing cooperation with the government. Like Papadopoulos and Flynn, Gates was caught lying to investigators and pleaded guilty. Gates played an important role within

Trump's inner circle—someone who understood the day-to-day operations of the campaign and worked on the postelection transition team, even maintaining a cozy relationship with the administration during the start of Trump's presidency. The information he shared bolstered the government's case against Manafort and aided the investigation into campaign staffers' criminal acts.

Gates and Manafort were indicted on October 27, 2017, on charges of conspiracy against the United States, conspiracy to launder money, acting as unregistered foreign agents, and making false statements. They were accused of acting as unregistered foreign agents for various Eastern European political entities between 2006 and 2015, generating millions of dollars that they funneled through corporations, offshore accounts, and other money laundering schemes. They were also indicted by a federal grand jury on February 22, 2018, in the Eastern District of Virginia. After Gates pleaded guilty to one charge of conspiracy against the United States and one charge of making false statements to the Special Counsel's Office and FBI agents in the District of Columbia, the additional charges against him were dismissed as part of his plea bargain.

Manafort initially maintained his innocence in court, but the move backfired. He was subsequently convicted by jury in a trial in the Eastern District of Virginia, then agreed to cooperate with Mueller's team to avoid the risk of a second conviction on the charges pending against him in Washington DC. After he continued to lie to Mueller's team, he was found in breach of his cooperation plea agreement, and he now faces more than seven years behind bars. Gates, meanwhile, chose to cooperate with investigators immediately following the indictment, flipping on his longtime friend in the process. Self-preservation is a significant motivator for defendants to cooperate with authorities and a powerful tool used to expose criminal enterprises and activity.

Throughout his career, Gates was comfortable serving in Manafort's shadow—the guy behind the guy. Richard William Gates III was born on April 27, 1972, in Fort Lee, Virginia, the son of Patricia Gates and army officer Richard W. Gates Jr. The family bounced around during Gates's childhood, living on military bases in Kentucky, North Carolina, and Germany. Gates eventually settled in Virginia after his father retired. He attended the College of William & Mary as an undergrad, earning a BA in government, and he later received a master's degree in public policy from George Washington University. Gates first crossed paths with his mentor in 1995 when he interned for Manafort's government and public relations firm, Black, Manafort, Stone and Kelly. After Manafort left the company, Gates continued to serve as a director until 1997, when he left to work in London for Gtech, leading the company's international business development program.

From 2000 to 2005 he served as partner and COO of Business Strategies and Insight, and he cofounded a public affairs and government relations firm, Capital Strategies, in 2003. He also worked at Scientific Games Corporation, where he was responsible for international business development and government relations.

After Manafort started a new firm, Davis Manafort Partners, Gates joined on in 2006, working across Eastern Europe and Africa with high-profile clients such as Ukrainian president Viktor Yanukovych. Now the protégé and mentor shared a more collaborative business relationship. The onetime intern had become a skilled practitioner in the world of international politics, business development, and global affairs.

National Politics

Gates entered national politics through his work with Manafort, working on two presidential nominating campaigns during the 1990s and early 2000s, Bob Dole and George W. Bush. Through lobbying efforts, Gates established relationships with figures such as Russian oligarch Oleg Deripaska, a close ally of President Vladimir Putin. Because of Gates's years spent operating in the shadows overseas and his subdued, no-nonsense personality, he remained relatively unknown in national political circles prior to joining Donald Trump's presidential campaign. But even if he lacked name recognition and wasn't as flashy as the ostrich jacket–wearing Manafort, Gates was a force and knew how to accomplish goals. Those traits would come in handy in his work with Trump's campaign and inauguration.

Involvement with the Trump Campaign

One month after Paul Manafort joined Trump's campaign in March 2016, Gates was added to the team. Both volunteered their services and weren't paid for their work on the campaign. Manafort saw an opportunity to ignite his languished career and build business relationships. Manafort's influence on the campaign created friction with campaign manager Corey Lewandowski, who saw him as a direct threat, especially after he was promoted to campaign chairman and chief strategist in May 2016. As the campaign faltered the following month, Trump made Manafort, the ultimate lobbyist, his new campaign manager. The goal: that the well-established Manafort would bring stability to a campaign that had endured numerous personnel changes and struggled to connect with GOP leaders and tried-and-true conservatives who were looking to back a more traditional candidate. But Manafort and Gates had trouble fully breaking free from the connections they had made in lobbying, specifically links in Ukraine and Russia.

Soon after joining the campaign, Gates, at Manafort's urging, began to send internal polling data to Konstantin Kilimnik, a longtime business colleague of Manafort's who authorities believe has connections to Russian intelligence. In the course of his cooperation, Gates confirmed that he used the encrypted app WhatsApp to send Kilimnik the polling data before deleting the messages. The plan, according to Robert Mueller's office, was for Kilimnik to share the data with contacts in Ukraine and Russia, including Oleg Deripaska. (Kilimnik, of course, disagrees with Mueller's assessment.)

By June 2016 Gates was running day-to-day operations for the Trump campaign, and he was fully entrenched in Team Trump at the Republican National Convention in mid-July, serving as the top Trump delegate wrangler and rubbing shoulders with Trump and his family as

Trump prepared to accept the party's nomination. But Gates became embroiled in a curious scandal after it emerged that a convention speech delivered by Trump's wife, Melania, had borrowed numerous lines from a 2008 address by First Lady Michelle Obama. While campaign insiders called out Gates in the media, saying he was overseeing the speech, Gates denied any involvement, and a longtime Trump ghost-writer, Meredith McIver, later took the blame.

Throughout the summer of 2016, the campaign had a bigger focus: finding thousands of Hillary Clinton's emails. Trump sent a signal to Moscow with a speech in early July: "Russia, if you're listening, I hope you're able to find the 30,000 emails that are missing." The emails had been saved to a private email server during Clinton's tenure as secretary of state. Trump's call for Clinton's emails set off a scramble. Gates later told the special counsel that Trump was "generally frustrated" that the emails hadn't been found. As the summer wore on, Gates said, the campaign "was planning a press strategy, a communications campaign, and messaging based on the possible release of Clinton emails by WikiLeaks. . . . Trump told Gates that more releases of damaging information would be coming."

Amid the search for dirt on Clinton, Manafort's shady dealings in Eastern Europe and Gates's participation came into focus. A series of critical articles highlighted the duo's work with pro-Russian political leaders in Ukraine, including lobbying in the United States on behalf of Ukrainian political leaders, questionable multimillion dollar payments, and failure to register as foreign agents under the Foreign Agents Registration Act, a felony. By August 17 Trump had announced a shake-up of his senior staff. Kellyanne Conway, a Republican pollster and Trump booster, would serve as campaign manager while Steve Bannon, an executive with the conservative website Breitbart News, was named chief executive. Conway projected a sense of unity, calling herself, Bannon, Manafort, and Gates the campaign's "core four." But the scandal-plagued Manafort was on the outside looking in. And just two days later, he resigned from the campaign. As Manafort stepped down, the Trump campaign announced that Gates would serve as its liaison to the Republican National Committee. Instead, Gates simply faded into the campaign's background.

Staffers at Trump Tower nicknamed Gates "The Walking Dead," since it was assumed Trump would sack Gates at his earliest convenience, and in fact at one point Trump reportedly ordered him gone. But somehow Gates survived. After Trump was elected, Gates helped plan and raise funds for the inauguration, and he was dubbed the inauguration's "shadow chair." The team raised $107 million, double the previous inauguration record, with reports swirling that foreign oligarchs may have paid big sums to receive access to Trump. The inaugural fund-raising activities and transactions are the subject of an investigation being led by the Southern District of New York.

Gates's perspectives working for the campaign and transition team have proven invaluable for authorities.

Investigation

The Department of Justice began investigating Gates and Manafort in September 2016, following the wave of media coverage about their lobbying work in Eastern Europe and failure to register as foreign agents. That investigation began eight months before Robert Mueller, the former FBI director, was named special counsel for the investigation into Russia's involvement with the 2016 election and connections with the Trump campaign.

Investigators found Manafort and Gates weren't truthful about their business dealings in letters sent to DOJ in November 2016 and February 2017, misrepresenting their efforts to connect two companies with an entity called the European Centre for Modern Ukraine and offering false statements about their unreported lobbying efforts.

FBI agents conducted a raid at Manafort's home in July 2017. Search warrants were also obtained for Manafort and Gates's email accounts, uncovering information that connected them to lobbying. In an October 27 indictment, prosecutors alleged that the duo "generated tens of millions of dollars in income" through their work in Ukraine and then laundered the money through various channels. Some of that money flowed through shell companies in Cyprus, Saint Vincent, the Grenadines, and Seychelles.

Some of the money was used to fund Manafort's lavish lifestyle, hidden away in offshore accounts and used to buy property that he then used as collateral to obtain loans. Gates used the ill-gotten money to "pay for his personal expenses, including his mortgage, children's tuition, and interior decorations of his Virginia residence," authorities said.

In January 2018, Gates told the Special Counsel's Office that according to Manafort, Trump's personal counsel told him they were "going to take care of us" and had urged Gates not to take a plea agreement. "We'll be taken care of," Manafort said. Gates asked Manafort if anyone mentioned the word "pardon." Manafort said no one had.

Gates was questioned by FBI agents on February 1, 2018, at the Special Counsel's Office. During that interview, according to Mueller's team, Gates lied about a March 19, 2013, meeting that involved Manafort, U.S. Rep. Dana Rohrabacher (R-CA), and former Rep. Vin Weber (R-MN), claiming that he was told "there were no discussions of Ukraine at the meeting." In actuality, Manafort and Weber had told Gates "the meeting went well," and Gates and Manafort had prepared a meeting for Ukraine leadership about the relevant topics discussed at the meeting. On February 22, 2018, a federal grand jury in Virginia returned the thirty-two-count indictment against the longtime business partners: sixteen counts of tax fraud for filing false individual income tax returns, seven counts of failure to file reports of foreign bank and financial accounts, five counts of conspiracy to commit bank fraud, and four counts of bank fraud. A superseding criminal information was also filed on February 2, 2018, against Gates in the District of Columbia charging him with two counts: a violation of Title 18 U.S.C. § 371 (conspiracy against the United States), and a violation of Title 18 U.S.C. § 1001 (making a false statement).

For the conspiracy charge, prosecutors focused on Gates helping

Manafort buy goods, services, and real estate from offshore accounts between 2008 and 2014 without paying taxes on that income, as well as hiding income by denoting overseas payments as "loans." Gates was cited for misleading Manafort's accountants by failing to disclose overseas accounts and income, as well as for hiding income from the IRS. Prosecutors also concentrated on Gates's failure to register as a foreign agent for his lobbying work in the Ukraine.

The conspiracy charge begs the question of how evidence of tax and bank fraud could amount to conspiring against the country. Gates's culpability for Count 1 of his cooperation plea agreement was well supported by the evidence of tax and bank fraud underlying the February 22, 2018, indictment against him and Manafort. The general conspiracy statute, Title 18 U.S.C. § 371, creates an offense "if two or more persons conspire either to commit any offense against the United States, or to defraud the United States, or any agency thereof in any manner or for any purpose." Violations of the "defraud clause" or "offense clause" require illegal agreement, criminal intent, and proof of an overt act.

Crimes that defraud the United States under Title 18 U.S.C. § 371 affect the government in at least one of three ways: they cheat the government out of money or property; they interfere with or obstruct legitimate government activity; or they make wrongful use of a governmental instrumentality.

Conspiracy, the illegal agreement element, was readily provable by the prosecution in that the investigation of the activities and transactions Manafort and Gates were involved in were ongoing agreements not to disclose their offshore income and further to hide their lobbying activities as foreign agents within the United States. While intent requires the impossible task of a visit into a defendant's mind at a given point in time, it was established here through circumstantial evidence: Gates repeatedly worked with Manafort to generate offshore income that he failed to report and pay taxes on. And time and time again, the pair engaged in lobbying activities for foreign agents, most notably Ukrainian president Viktor Yanukovych and his Party of Regions.

In Gates's case, the fraudulent activity spanned at least six years. Each time tax returns were filed, the offshore income was *not* disclosed and taxes on that income were evaded, an overt act toward completion of the conspiracy (illegal agreement) to defraud the Internal Revenue Service, an agency of the United States. Furthermore, each time Gates engaged in lobbying activity, no matter what the scope, and failed to register as a foreign agent, he engaged in fraud by omission. Gates's tax fraud was a crime against the United States because it "cheated the government" out of money—the taxes on Gates's offshore income. In addition, his failure to register as a foreign agent defrauded the government in that it interfered with and obstructed a "legitimate government activity," namely, the monitoring of foreign agents and their activities within U.S. soil to protect national security.

Count 2 of Gates's cooperation plea agreement is similarly well supported by evidence uncovered in the Mueller investigation. Lying to authorities is an ongoing theme among the defendants whose conduct is analyzed in this book. They were *all* charged with violations of Title 18 U.S.C. § 1001, which prohibits making a false statement to a specific branch of government (in Gates's case, the FBI); it also requires that the defendant acted willfully and that the statements were material to the agency's decisions or activities. Gates's misstating the 2013 meeting involving Manafort was not the only lie he told investigators, but it was the lie used as the factual basis for his plea. On February 23, 2018, Gates pleaded guilty to the conspiracy and false statement charges, and the remaining counts in the indictment were dismissed.

Bound by his cooperation plea agreement, in August 2018 Gates testified against Manafort, providing damning details about their years of tax evasion, shell companies, and money laundering that helped lead to Manafort's conviction. The testimony was also damaging for Gates, who was forced to admit under oath that he had carried on an extramarital affair about a decade earlier at his London apartment and that he had embezzled several hundred thousand dollars from Manafort.

It may have all had little to do with Donald Trump's campaign, but Gates's cooperation plea agreement and Manafort's conviction gave tremendous credibility to Robert Mueller's investigation. The investigation couldn't be ignored, and it was not a "hoax" or a "witch hunt." Nor was it going away.

Sentence

More than a year after Rick Gates pleaded guilty, he hadn't been sentenced because he was still cooperating "with respect to several ongoing investigations," according to a March 2019 joint status report to the U.S. District Court in Washington. The status report requested a sixty-day delay, with the parties set to reconvene. No other details were provided about the nature and scope of the information Gates was providing or the investigations he was aiding.

Once sentenced, Gates could go home on probation or go to prison. The maximum sentence he faces for the two counts of conviction is ten years (five years per count). A maximum statutory sentence isn't expected. Rather, in reaching a fair sentence for Gates, the judge will use the U.S. Federal Sentencing Guidelines, an advisory sentencing guide, along with considering Gates's "3553 factors," mitigating characteristics under Title 18 U.S.C. § 3553.

Under the guidelines, Gates's sentencing range is fifty-seven to seventy-one months. His cooperation plea agreement and all of the information surrounding his case indicate that the judge will consider a sentence at the low end of this range, fifty-seven months. While Gates could potentially serve the majority of fifty-seven or more months behind bars at a Bureau of Prisons facility, the likelihood of that is slim. This is largely due to the scope and extent of Gates's cooperation despite his initial lack of candor.

Notably, under Gates's cooperation plea agreement, the prosecutors are bound to bring a "5K1.1 motion" at Gates's sentencing. Section 5K1.1 of the guidelines provides that "upon motion of the government [attorneys] stating that the defendant has provided 'substantial assistance' in the investigation or prosecution of another person who has committed an offense, the court may depart from the guidelines." In Gates's case, the judge may sentence him from no prison time (below the guidelines range), within the guidelines range, or up to the statutory maximum of ten years (above the guidelines range). Given Gates's cooperation, a sentence within or above the guidelines range is highly unlikely.

This is because Gates's cooperation stretched more than a year, even beyond the release of the Mueller Report in April 2019. He met with investigators dozens of times. He suited up, showed up, and testified against Manafort at his trial. At a minimum he helped secure a conviction against Manafort, a verdict which contributed to Manafort's decision to plead guilty in a second trial. Gates's cooperation is no doubt an example of "substantial assistance" that warrants a below-guideline sentence, but how much lower than fifty-seven months? Could that mean no prison time and probation, or will Gates see the inside of a prison cell? Gates has no criminal history, and prior to the case he was seen as living an upstanding life. He's provided "substance assistance" to the government as part of a cooperation plea agreement. He has accepted responsibility by agreeing to plead early and avoiding an undue waste of government resources. His big picture is of a good man who did bad things in association with bad people.

While the judge could most definitely use her broad discretion to sentence Gates to probation and no time in prison, the sentencing trend in the cases stemming from the Mueller investigation is that everyone serves time, even if symbolic and minimal such as the two-week sentence issued to foreign policy advisor George Papadopoulos. Rick Gates played a much bigger role with the campaign than the "coffee boy," but they both found themselves in hot water after lying to investigators, and when caught, they chose to cooperate.

Gates's case demonstrated early on that Mueller's team was looking at everything, even business deals and financial transactions not related to the Trump campaign and its conspiracy or coordination with Russia to interfere with the 2016 elections.

CHAPTER 4

PAUL MANAFORT

THE LOBBYIST IN THE OSTRICH JACKET

★ ★ ★ ★ ★

Association: Campaign manager, 2016 Trump campaign

Crimes: *Eastern District of Virginia*: guilty by verdict of five counts of violating Title 26 U.S.C. § 7206 (tax fraud), two counts of violating Title 18 U.S.C. § 1344 (bank fraud), one count of violating Title 31 U.S.C. § 5314 (failure to file a report of foreign bank and financial accounts)

   District of Columbia: guilty by plea to one count of violating Title 18 U.S.C. § 371 (conspiracy against the United States), one count of violating Title 18 U.S.C. § 371 (conspiracy to obstruct justice)

Sentence: *Eastern District of Virginia*: 47 months; *District of Columbia*: 73 months. Sentences running partially concurrently for a total of 7.5 years

Paul Manafort most definitely thought he was above the law.

The longtime lobbyist and political consultant shifted from one cause to the next for decades, guided not by morality but by power and money. He helped a generation of Republicans reach the White House. He befriended despots and tried to make them more relatable to the western world, lobbying efforts that in some cases led to further fighting and strife in war-torn countries. Manafort lived a lavish lifestyle that for years was illegally funded, relying on a complex system of offshore money, improperly obtained loans, and tax fraud to buy things and replenish his bank accounts. And when his illicit activities finally came to light and his closest colleagues had turned against him, he still wouldn't stop lying. His web of crimes and deceit, as well as his stubbornness, turned a kingmaker into federal inmate #35207-016.

Manafort was involved with some of the most notable aspects of Donald Trump's campaign, events that cemented or fueled intrigue about the campaign's connections with Russia and played a significant role in the special counsel's investigation. It was a stunning fall for a smooth operator who spent his career building winning campaigns and skating trouble whenever it arose.

Paul John Manafort Jr., was born in Connecticut on April 1, 1949. He drew inspiration from his father, who helped run his family's construction company, Manafort Brothers. Manafort Sr. served as the mayor of the town of New Britain in the 1960s and 1970s and worked other government jobs such as state public works commissioner. In the early 1980s, the father was accused of perjury as part of a corruption investigation, but the charges were eventually dropped. By that point, Paul Jr. had become a colorful figure in his own right.

National Politics

Paul Manafort attended Georgetown University in Washington DC, completing his undergraduate studies in 1971 and graduating from law school in 1974. He soon found himself in Gerald Ford's administration as a staff assistant for national security and justice in the Presidential Personnel Office from 1975 to 1977. He also served as Ford's regional and delegate coordinator in the 1976 election, which the Republican lost to Jimmy Carter. Through the Young Republican National Federation, an influential group for Republicans between ages eighteen and forty, Manafort and a fellow up-and-coming GOP devotee, Roger Stone, galvanized their influence and dirty tricks. Manafort backed Stone's bid for group chair in 1977, and Stone was elected. Manafort and Stone had recognized the Republican sea change and shifted to Reagan's camp.

Manafort and Stone positioned themselves to play influential roles in Reagan's 1980 campaign. Manafort served as convention deputy political director and southern political coordinator for the California politician and former actor, who ultimately defeated Carter and made it to the White House. But instead of taking White House jobs after Reagan was elected, Manafort and Stone opened a lobbying and political consulting firm with GOP campaign veteran Charles Black. There was more money to be made this way. The lobbying wing of their firm, Black, Manafort, Stone and Kelly, was headed by Peter Kelly, a Democratic fund-raiser, while Black, Manafort, Stone and Atwater focused on consulting (Lee Atwater was Reagan's deputy campaign manager for his 1984 reelection). Money flowed in from everywhere: from straight-laced politicians and overseas dictators to major corporations. By the early 1980s, even a Manhattan real estate developer named Donald Trump was a client of Manafort's firm.

The firm represented such figures as Philippines despot Ferdinand Marcos and Angola guerilla leader Jonas Savimbi. Manafort also represented corrupt leaders in Kenya and Nigeria and a prime minister in the Bahamas who was the focus of a DEA drug trafficking investigation. Meanwhile, Manafort and Stone embodied the decadence that defined the 1980s, using their six-figure salaries to fuel their affinity for tailor-made suits.

During the decade, Manafort had cemented his role as a kingmaker, helping place Ronald Reagan and George H. W. Bush in the White House. But as the 1980s wore down, his firm's multipronged approach and courting of controversy drew congressional attention. Manafort was forced to appear before a House committee after his development firm was awarded more than $31 million in federal subsidies for a New Jersey Housing and Urban Development project, and his firm was paid $326,000 in consulting fees. He told Congress his efforts amounted to "influence-peddling," a role that he would continue to carry out in the years and decades that followed.

By 1995 Manafort had launched a new consulting firm, DMS Inc. in Alexandria, Virginia. A year later the firm was known as Davis, Manafort and Freedman, and Manafort was back in the national spotlight, overseeing the Republican National Convention in San Diego, this time backing Bob Dole's presidential nomination.

A decade later, when Manafort's stateside influence had dimmed, he looked to Ukraine and Russia for new lobbying opportunities. Still working with Davis Manafort Partners, he connected with Ukrainian politician Viktor Yanukovych and Oleg Deripaska, a Russian oligarch with close ties to Russian president Vladimir Putin. Deripaska sent millions of dollars to Manafort for his lobbying efforts, some of which vanished. Meanwhile, Manafort helped the pro-Russian Yanukovych become Ukraine's president in 2010. He also worked with Konstantin Kilimnik, who is presumed to be a Russian operative. While Manafort fostered these relationships in the public view, he failed to report them in lobbying filings to the U.S. government.

Notably Rick Gates, the Virginia-born lobbyist who had interned years earlier with Black, Manafort, Stone and Kelly, became one of the firm's most loyal employees, playing a major role with the firm. By 2014 Manafort's relationship with Deripaska had soured over a failed investment deal, and Yanukovych was driven from power. With Manafort's business in Europe languishing, he struggled to maintain his lavish lifestyle. He was looking for the next big score, something to revive his career. And suddenly a familiar name from his past emerged as a 2016 presidential contender, Donald Trump.

Involvement with the Trump Campaign

Manafort and Trump had known each other since the 1970s thanks to an introduction by cold-blooded lawyer Roy Cohn. They ran in similar social circles and were roughly the same age. As Trump's White House run galvanized in early 2016, he hoped to fend off attacks from other candidates and secure his party's nomination. Trump needed a delegate-wrangler, something Manafort had done effectively since the 1970s. Manafort was recommended to Trump by two mutual friends, businessman Tom Barrack and Roger Stone.

Manafort's association with Trump and his campaign added

credibility to the candidacy: he was a known commodity for a campaign that had struggled to find stability. In late March 2016 Manafort was announced as leading Trump's delegate-corralling efforts in an unpaid role. He saw it as a chance to reinvigorate his career. One month later, he brought along Gates, his trusted sidekick. The goal was to reach the 1,237 delegates needed to secure the nomination, fighting off challenges posed by other Republican candidates. But Manafort didn't take long to assert his presence on the campaign, quickly gaining Trump's trust and calling the candidate by his first name. In May Manafort was named campaign chairman and chief strategist, creating a power struggle with campaign manager Corey Lewandowski. In June Manafort was named campaign manager, and Lewandowski was forced to the sidelines.

Manafort's tenure as campaign manager coincided with numerous overtures with Russia—incidents that were detailed in Special Counsel Robert Mueller's March 2019 report. Specifically, after joining the campaign, Manafort began sending internal polling data to Kilimnik, his former employee with Kremlin connections, with the belief that the data was being forwarded to Deripaska. Manafort and Kilimnik also met in New York on August 2, 2016, days after Gates met with Deripaska in Moscow.

On June 9, Manafort, Donald Trump Jr., and Jared Kushner attended the infamous Trump Tower meeting with a Russian lawyer in hopes that they would obtain "official documents and information that would incriminate" Hillary Clinton, the 2016 Democratic presidential candidate. During the meeting, Kushner sent a message to Manafort: "Waste of time."

Around that same time, it was also announced that Russian hackers had infiltrated the DNC, emails that Trump's team had spent months trying to track down. According to Rick Gates, Manafort was "excited" about the emails potentially being released.

The summer of 2016 was also significant, as Manafort's past business connections in Europe would come back to haunt him. A ledger was uncovered showing $12.7 million in cash payments from Viktor

Yanukovych's Party of Regions to Manafort between 2007 and 2012. At the time, Manafort called the possibility that he received cash payments "unfounded, silly, and nonsensical." Trump, seeking to diminish his exposure to the scandal, decided to reshuffle the campaign's senior staff, with Manafort staying on as chairman and Kellyanne Conway and Steve Bannon elevated to campaign manager and CEO, respectively. Manafort's firm's lobbying effort on behalf of Ukraine's ruling party and Manafort and Gates failing to register as foreign agents were also revealed. On August 19, 2016, Manafort decided to bow out of the campaign. Trump released a statement following Manafort's resignation, calling him a "true professional" and wishing him "the greatest success."

Investigation

In September 2016, the Department of Justice launched an investigation into Manafort and Gates's lobbying work in Ukraine. Having found the pair untruthful in letters about their lobbying work and business connections, FBI agents carried out a raid at Manafort's Virginia home in July 2017, seizing documents and financial records. The raid revealed a $10 million loan from Deripaska to Manafort, a loan that was never repaid, among numerous other offshore transactions that had been hidden from the government and never reported as income. The raid demonstrated that Special Counsel Robert Mueller meant business!

Crime and Cooperation

District of Columbia

On October 27, 2017, a grand jury in the District of Columbia indicted Manafort on nine counts: conspiracy against the United States, conspiracy to launder money, four counts of failure to file reports of foreign bank and financial accounts covering the years 2011 to 2014, one count of unregistered agent of a foreign principal, false and misleading FARA (Foreign Agents Registration Act) statements, and making false statements. The indictment alleged that Manafort laundered more than $18 million, using offshore money to buy property, goods, and services and that he "used his hidden overseas wealth to enjoy a lavish lifestyle in the United States, without paying taxes on that income."

Authorities further alleged that Manafort, through a holding company, bought a condo in New York City for $2.85 million using unreported money and applied for a mortgage, falsely claiming it was a secondary home used by his daughter and son-in-law, when in fact he was renting out the condo on Airbnb and "charging thousands of dollars a week." He also obtained a "construction loan" for a different property, but instead of renovations and repairs, he used the money to make a down payment for a property in California.

Simultaneous to the indictment against Manafort and Gates, it was revealed that Mueller had secured his first guilty plea in the investigation, foreign policy advisor George Papadopoulos, for making false statements to FBI agents. Manafort's attorney called the charges "ridiculous" and said there was "no evidence" that the longtime lobbyist or the Trump campaign colluded with Russia in its interference with the 2016 election.

As Manafort maintained his innocence, in February 2018 a Washington DC grand jury returned an indictment charging Manafort, assisted by Gates, of solicitation of two U.S. lobbying firms on behalf of Yanukovych, the Party of Regions, and the government of Ukraine. Manafort was also accused of organizing a group of influential European leaders, dubbed the Hapsburg Group, to lobby in the United States and Europe on behalf of Ukraine. Based on these allegations, he was charged with conspiracy against the United States for failing to file proper financial disclosure forms with the Departments of Justice and the Treasury; conspiracy to launder money; unregistered agent of a foreign principal; false or misleading FARA statements; and making false statements.

In the days following the indictment, Manafort and his Russia-connected former business colleague, Konstantin Kilimnik, contacted two PR officials connected to the Hapsburg Group. Manafort sent one of the PR reps an article about the Hapsburg Group using an encrypted app. "We should talk," Manafort wrote, suggesting that the Hapsburg

Group only had worked in Europe, not the United States. The potential witness, who had not spoken to Manafort in years, told the government that he viewed the contact as an effort to "suborn perjury." Kilimnik followed with similar messages of his own. These attempts by Manafort and Kilimnik to tamper with witnesses led to the filing of a superseding indictment on June 8, 2018, in Washington DC, where both men were charged with two counts of obstructing justice.

The depth of Manafort's legal turmoil was reflected by the range of charging documents he faced, adding new charges to an already long list of alleged crimes. An indictment is a charging document that follows a grand jury finding that probable cause exists that a crime was committed and that the defendant committed the crime. A superseding indictment replaces a previously issued indictment when new evidence is obtained in support of new charges. An indictment and superseding indictment are both issued by a grand jury upon finding probable cause that the defendant committed the crime(s). Much like an indictment, an information is another type of charging document that contains charges against a defendant along with the supporting factual basis. Unlike an indictment, an information does not require a vote by grand jury.

In Manafort's case, it was in fact a two-count superseding information that marked Robert Mueller's final charges against him. On September 14, 2018, weeks after being found guilty of eight counts in the Eastern District of Virginia, Manafort pleaded guilty to the superseding information pursuant to a cooperation plea agreement. The man who not long before was urging his sidekick to stay strong and fight the charges was not only pleading guilty himself but also agreeing to cooperate and provide substantial assistance to the Mueller team. He pleaded guilty to a violation of Title 18 U.S.C. § 371, conspiracy against the United States—a charge consisting of tax fraud, Foreign Bank and Financial Accounts (FBAR) crimes, FARA violations, and false statements to the Department of Justice—as well as a second violation of this law, conspiracy to obstruct justice, for tampering with two witnesses, a violation of Title 18 U.S.C. § 1512. Under the terms of his plea agreement, Manafort agreed to "cooperate fully, truthfully, completely, and forthrightly" with the government, and any breach of the obligations by Manafort would render the deal invalid. "It's a tough day for Mr. Manafort, but he's accepted responsibility," his lawyer said.

Much like Rick Gates, Manafort pleaded guilty to the conspiracy charge based on the ample evidence that the prosecutors had to prove him guilty beyond a reasonable doubt at trial. As discussed earlier, crimes that defraud the United States under Title 18 U.S.C. § 371 affect the government in at least one of three ways: they cheat the government out of money or property; they interfere or obstruct legitimate government activity; or they make wrongful use of a governmental instrumentality.

With Gates cooperating and having pleaded guilty to this charge, prosecutors had more than sufficient evidence to prove the illegal agreement (conspiracy) between Manafort and Gates for their pattern of failing to report their lobbying activities and their hiding of millions of dollars of income so that it would go undetected and untaxed. And time and time again, Manafort engaged in lobbying activities for foreign agents, most notably Ukrainian president Viktor Yanukovych and his Party of Regions while failing to maintain records of and report his activities as a foreign agent. Much like Gates, Manafort pleaded guilty because he was in fact guilty of conspiracy against the United States: the millions of dollars Manafort failed to report as income on his taxes and his continued obstruction of legitimate government activity in connection with his failures to properly report his lobbying as a foreign agent defrauded the U.S. government in more ways than one.

In his cooperation plea agreement, Manafort pleaded guilty to a second violation of Title 18 U.S.C. § 371 for an underlying violation of Title 18 U.S.C. § 1512, obstruction of justice, specifically witness tampering. Under Section 1512(b), "whoever knowingly . . . corruptly persuades another person, or attempts to do so, or engages in misleading conduct toward another person, with intent to influence, delay, or prevent the testimony of any person in an official proceeding" is guilty of witness tampering.

Manafort's text messages and phone records—part of the special counsel's overwhelming evidence—revealed Manafort's communications with two PR reps who knew of his lobbying efforts in the United States involving the Hapsburg Group. Manafort, in collaboration with his Russia-connected colleague Kilimnik, reached out to the two potential witnesses, hoping to influence their account of the facts and ensure that any statements or testimony they provide would be advantageous to Manafort.

A defendant is guilty of obstruction of justice if he engages in witness tampering: the influencing or attempted influencing of a witness's testimony at an official proceeding. The fact that the two PR reps failed to comply with Manafort's direct and indirect messages does not absolve Manafort in any way. A mere attempt to influence a witness is a crime. Manafort had conspired with Kilimnik to influence two witnesses in connection with the investigation of his lobbying activities on behalf of Ukraine. He pleaded guilty to obstruction of justice because he was in fact guilty of the crime.

By November 2018 the Special Counsel's Office had caught Manafort lying to investigators numerous times, including about his interactions and a meeting with Kilimnik, Kilimnik's role in the witness tampering in Manafort's Washington DC case, a $125,000 payment to a firm that had worked for Manafort in 2017, another Department of Justice investigation, and his contact with the Trump administration. Manafort told investigators that he stopped communicating with Trump's administration in February 2018, but communications had continued and included a May 2018 text exchange in which Manafort "authorized a person to speak with an Administration official on Manafort's behalf." In the government's December 7, 2018, submission in support of its breach determination, Mueller stated that Manafort told "multiple discernible lies—these were not instances of mere memory lapses." The Special Counsel's Office was done working with Manafort.

Eastern District of Virginia

On February 22, 2018, a grand jury in the Eastern District of Virginia filed a thirty-two-count indictment against the business partners, alleging that Manafort, with Gates's help, filed false tax returns, failed to file reports of foreign bank and financial accounts, conspired to commit bank fraud, and committed bank fraud. These charges were based on evidence that between 2015 and early 2017, after Yanukovych fled to Russia and their income from the Ukraine dwindled, Manafort and Gates "fraudulently secured more than twenty million dollars in loans by falsely inflating Manafort's and his company's income and by failing to disclose existing debt in order to qualify for loans." One day after the indictment was filed, Gates pleaded guilty to making false statements to FBI agents, agreeing to cooperate with Mueller's team in exchange for the remaining charges against him being dismissed. Manafort, however, wasn't cooperating so readily, stating, "I had hoped and expected my business colleague would have had the strength to continue the battle to prove our innocence. For reasons yet to surface he chose to do otherwise."

Manafort's trial in the Eastern District of Virginia began on July 31. The three-week trial forced him to face off against Gates, the government's star witness. Prosecutors highlighted Manafort's spending habits, including $1.2 million on suits and $15,000 for an ostrich skin jacket. On Day 6 of the trial, Gates—who declined to look at Manafort in the courtroom—testified about his efforts to conceal millions of dollars on his mentor's behalf and falsify documents so Manafort could secure loans. He also testified about secret bank accounts in Cyprus, St. Vincent, and the Grenadines. "I'm here to tell the truth," Gates said.

The trial also featured Manafort's tax preparer, who under an immunity deal testified about having helped disguise Manafort's foreign income as a loan. On August 21, 2018, a Virginia jury found Manafort guilty on eight counts: five counts of violating Title 26 U.S.C. § 7206 (tax fraud), two counts of violating Title 18 U.S.C. § 1344 (bank fraud), and one count of violating Title 31 U.S.C. § 5314 (failure to file a report of foreign bank and financial accounts). Title 26 U.S.C. § 7206 enumerates a number of instances in which an individual may be in violation of the law. One such instance requires proof beyond a reasonable doubt that the defendant willfully made and subscribed to any tax return, statement, or other document under the penalty of perjury, which he does not believe to be true and correct as to every material fact. Prosecutors presented substantial evidence of at least five instances from 2010 to 2014 when Manafort had filed tax returns containing information he knew to be false. The filing of tax returns known to contain false information is tax fraud.

Any individual who knowingly engages in or attempts to engage in any scheme to defraud a financial institution or obtain funds, credits, or other property owned by or in the custody of a financial institution by means of false or fraudulent pretenses, representations, or pretenses is guilty of bank fraud, a violation of Title 18 U.S.C. § 1344. Manafort was found guilty of bank fraud charges connected to a $3.4 million Citizens Bank loan and a $1 million Bank of California loan.

Title 31 U.S.C. § 5314 requires residents and citizens of the United States to keep records and file records when the resident/citizen makes a transaction or maintains a relation for any person with a foreign financial agency. The records and reports must contain the identity and address of the participants to the transaction or relationship, the legal capacity in which the individual is acting, the identity of the beneficiaries to the transaction, and a description of the transaction. Having failed to file an FBAR report in 2012, Manafort was in clear violation of this law.

A mistrial was declared on the remaining ten charges, which involved Manafort's alleged failure to file FBARs in 2011, 2013, and 2014, as well as the conspiracy to commit bank fraud and bank fraud charges. When a jury cannot reach a verdict, a mistrial is declared. Prosecutors then have the discretion to refile and prosecute the charges again. Double jeopardy does not prohibit prosecution following a mistrial, since no verdict was reached. In Manafort's case, the Special Counsel's Office chose not to re-indict Manafort on the ten counts he was spared by the jury.

President Trump remained supportive of Manafort following his conviction: "I must tell you that Paul Manafort is a good man," Trump said. "He was with Ronald Reagan. He was with a lot of different people over the years. And I feel very sad about that. It doesn't involve me, but I still feel—you know, it's a very sad thing that happened. This has nothing to do with Russian collusion. This started as Russian collusion. This has absolutely nothing to do—this is a witch hunt, and it's a disgrace."

A guilty verdict and a guilty plea in Manafort's cases were not the end of his criminal exposure. Moments after Manafort was sentenced in Washington DC in March 2019, the Manhattan District Attorney's Office announced a sixteen-count grand jury indictment against him. There he faces three counts of residential mortgage fraud, attempt to commit residential mortgage fraud, three counts of conspiracy, eight counts of falsifying business records, and schemes to defraud, crimes that were allegedly committed between 2015 and 2017 and involved, among other things, Manafort using false information to obtain more than $1 million in mortgage loans.

Sentence

Eastern District of Virginia

The tax and bank fraud counts in Virginia came with a sentencing guideline range of nineteen to twenty-four years. But on March 8, 2019, Manafort was sentenced to only forty-seven months in prison and fined $50,000. The sentence was extraordinary and stirred national debate as to fairness and disparity.

District of Columbia

In a February 23, 2019, sentencing memo in the District of Columbia case, Mueller suggested that Manafort presented a "grave risk of recidivism." On March 13 Manafort was sentenced to seventy-three months on the two violations of Title U.S.C. § 371 in his failed cooperation plea agreement: conspiracy against the United States based on tax fraud, FBAR crimes, FARA violations, false statements to the Department of Justice, and conspiracy against the United States for obstruction of justice (witness tampering). Thirty of the seventy-three months run concurrently with his sentence in the Eastern District of Virginia. All told, Manafort is sentenced to ninety months (7.5 years) in prison. And based on federal sentencing rules, Manafort is expected to serve 85 percent of this time behind bars. Given his age and deteriorating health, this could mean the rest of Manafort's life.

Under Title 18 U.S.C. § 3553, the court "shall impose a sentence sufficient, but not greater than necessary" to deter and punish while considering "the nature and circumstances of the offense and the [individual] history and characteristics of the defendant." Then at sentencing, a federal judge considers both aggravating and mitigating factors to reach a fair sentence. Individual characteristics of the defendant such as age and health are mitigating factors that are considered to potentially reduce a defendant's sentence. Manafort's age and deteriorating health were the two primary mitigating factors argued in his favor at sentencing. The normally suit-clad Manafort, nearly seventy years old, had begun showing up to court in a wheelchair. His legal team claimed that Manafort had been suffering from depression, anxiety, and gout.

Like many of the crimes included in this work, the bulk of Manafort's offenses were unrelated to Mueller's investigation of collusion with Russian officials to influence the 2016 elections. When federal agents conduct an investigation, they often encounter criminal conduct unrelated to the subject matter of the investigation. Mueller's strategy, a common one, was to indict on charges related to his investigation and refer unrelated charges to the appropriate branches of the Department of Justice for further investigation, indictment, and prosecution. By mounting any and all charges for which authorities have evidence, prosecutors increase their leverage in muscling a defendant into providing information relevant not only to the investigation at hand but as to other investigations as well.

In Manafort's case, facing twenty-five counts in two districts was sound strategy by Mueller to sway him into ultimately agreeing to enter into a cooperation plea agreement with the Mueller team. But Manafort breached his plea agreement by misleading the prosecutors and lying about material facts. He failed to provide substantial assistance and cooperate fully. Had Manafort instead candidly and fully cooperated with the Mueller team, it would be reasonable to assume that the chairman of the Trump campaign, who was in such close contact with Russian officials such as Kilimnik, sharing polling data from the elections could in fact provide substantial assistance directly related to the investigation of Russian interference. So before you dismiss Manafort's financial crimes as being unrelated to the issue of collusion with Russia, remember his role and proximity to Trump and his campaign, as well as his abundant ties with Russia—ties that he still couldn't tell the truth about even after he agreed to cooperate with Mueller.

Through Mueller's efforts, the kingmaker had fallen and his lavish lifestyle had been turned upside down by a series of crimes and deceit. Notably, while Trump could issue a pardon for his former campaign manager, the presidential pardon power does not extend to charges pending against Manafort in New York. Manafort is serving his 7.5-year sentence at Federal Correctional Institution in Loretto, Pennsylvania, with an expected release date of December 25, 2024.

CHAPTER 5

MICHAEL COHEN

THE FIXER WHO FLIPPED

★ ★ ★ ★ ★

Association: Donald Trump's personal attorney; Trump Organization executive vice president

Crimes: *Southern District of New York*: Guilty by plea to eight counts, five counts of violating Title 26 U.S.C. § 7201 (tax evasion), one count of violating Title 18 U.S.C. § 1014 (false statements to a financial institution), one count of violating Title 52 U.S.C. § 30118(a) and Title 52 U.S.C. § 30109(d)(1)(A), and Title 18 U.S.C. § 2(b) (unlawful campaign contributions), one count of violating Title 52 U.S.C. § 30116(a)(1)(A), Title 52 U.S.C. §§ 30116(a)(7) and 30109(d)(l)(A), and Title 18 U.S.C. § 2(b) (excessive campaign contribution)

    Southern District of New York (Special Counsel's Office): Guilty by plea to one count of violating Title 18 U.S.C. § 1001 (a)(2) (false statements)

Sentence: *Southern District of New York*: thirty-six months in prison; *Southern District of New York (Special Counsel's Office)*: two months in prison. Sentences running concurrently.

Michael Cohen once bragged that he would take a bullet for his boss, Donald Trump. But on February 27, 2019, he was singing a different tune, telling Congress under oath that Trump was a racist, a conman, and a cheat. "I regret the day I said 'yes' to Mr. Trump. I regret all the help and support I gave him along the way," Cohen said.

Trump's longtime fixer has been known as a bully and a henchman, someone who would do anything to further the Trump family's business and personal interests, even if that involved threats and intimidation—a pitbull. Some have even compared Cohen to Tom Hagen, Vito Corleone's consigliore in the *Godfather* movies.

Michael Dean Cohen was born August 25, 1966, the son of Maurice, a surgeon who survived the Holocaust, and Sondra, a nurse, and he grew up on New York's Long Island. After graduating from American University and Thomas M. Cooley Law School, he practiced as an attorney for multiple law firms.

Cohen first connected with Donald Trump Jr. and joined the Trump Organization in 2006 when the condo building where he lived was trying to remove the name "Trump." He rallied residents and got the board of directors removed. Soon afterward, he was hired as the Trump Organization's executive vice president and special counsel to Donald Trump. Cohen left the company as Trump took office in January 2017. While people close to Cohen say he was frustrated at being turned down for a job at the White House, Cohen maintains he never wanted a job in the administration. Regardless of why Cohen didn't make it to Washington in January 2017, he became Trump's personal attorney and seemingly hit the jackpot by picking up consulting opportunities due to his proximity to Trump, raking in millions of dollars from overseas sources and corporations. The reward for Cohen's meager efforts included wire payments from AT&T to the tune of $550,000, and another $600,000 from a South Korean company that produces and sells aircraft to the Department of Defense. Cohen also began receiving monthly payments of $83,333 from Columbus Nova LLC, an investment management firm with connections to Russian national Viktor Vekselberg, who has ties to Vladimir Putin and was sanctioned for interference with the 2016 U.S. elections.

Having set up Essential Consultants, LLC in October 2016 just weeks before the election to pay off a porn star threatening to reveal a 2006 tryst with candidate Trump, Cohen received money wired into this account for his "consulting" work.

National Politics

Cohen served as Trump's chief political advisor in 2011 when the real estate developer considered a run for the White House (he ultimately declined to run at the time). Cohen created a website for Trump—www .ShouldTrumpRun.com—and flew to Iowa to meet with Republican Party officials. During the 2016 campaign, although Cohen had no formal title with the Trump campaign, he served as an advisor, used a campaign email address, and made numerous media appearances in support of his longtime client.

In April 2017 Cohen was named the deputy finance chair of the Republican National Committee's Finance Committee, but he stepped down from the position in June 2018 when the Special Counsel's Office investigation intensified.

Involvement with the Trump Campaign

Michael Cohen played a significant role in Trump's election efforts, working tirelessly to kill damaging stories about Trump, including accounts by two women who claimed they had sexual encounters or affairs with Trump a decade earlier. The women, adult film star Stormy Daniels, and model and Playboy Playmate Karen McDougal, had salacious stories that could have damaged Trump's chances in the election. Stories of Trump's sexual conquests were nothing new; his affair with his second wife, Marla Maples, was a tabloid news fixation years earlier, and the jet-setting real estate tycoon was known for his womanizing ways almost as much as for his hosting *The Apprentice* or his use of his last name to brand everything from casino resorts to planes, steaks, and alcohol. The encounters mattered not because of their salacious nature. Trump's affairs while married were not crimes or concerns in any investigation of wrongdoing against our nation. Rather, the significance of the Daniels and McDougal stories was that ahead of the 2016 election, Cohen secured both women's silence, one through a bank transfer and the other as part of a tabloid "catch and kill" scheme to protect a presidential candidate. Notably, prosecutors uncovered that not only did Cohen buy the women's silence to protect candidate Trump but he did so at Trump's direction in violation of campaign finance laws. In their December 7, 2018, sentencing memo, prosecutors indicated that Cohen had admitted to having "acted in coordination with and at the direction of Individual-1," referring to Donald Trump. And while campaign finance laws are generally favorable to the candidate, Cohen and Trump managed to violate it not once but twice—once in the case of McDougal, and again regarding Daniels.

The "catch and kill" deal with McDougal was born out of an August 2015 meeting with Cohen, Trump, and David Pecker, CEO of American Media, which owns the *National Enquirer.* At the crux of the meeting was Pecker's offer to suppress negative stories related to women claiming extramarital affairs with Trump.

During the summer of 2016, Pecker was tipped off about McDougal shopping her story of an affair with Trump. With no intention of ever publishing McDougal's story and at Cohen's insistence, AMI began negotiating with the former Playboy model, eventually agreeing to pay $150,000 and offer her a two-magazine commitment for her silence. A pro at setting up shell companies, Cohen incorporated "Resolution Consultants LLC" with the specific purpose of paying AMI for the McDougal deal. On September 20, 2018, AMI and the SDNY reached a non-prosecution agreement in which AMI admitted making the $150,000 payment "in concert with a candidate's presidential campaign, and in order to ensure that the woman did not publicize damaging allegations about the candidate before the 2016 presidential election." "Candidate" referred to Donald Trump and "the woman" was Karen McDougal. In fact, in late July 2018, CNN's Chris Cuomo obtained a stunning audio recording of Trump and Cohen discussing McDougal. "I need to open up a company for the transfer of all of that info regarding our friend David," Cohen said, referring to Pecker. The pair were heard discussing the details of financing. "Pay with cash," Trump told Cohen. The recording was irrefutable ironclad proof that Trump was not only aware of the payment but had helped orchestrate it.

Closer to the election on October 8, 2016, amid fallout from a 2005 recording featuring Trump talking about taking advantage of women, which came to be infamously known as the *"Access Hollywood* tape," a rep for Stormy Daniels, whose real name is Stephanie Clifford, reached out to an editor at AMI's *National Enquirer* and suggested Daniels was ready to go public with her allegations of a 2006 tryst with Trump during a golf tournament in Lake Tahoe, California. Although Pecker immediately alerted Cohen of this news, he wasn't interested in buying Daniels's story. According to Cohen, when he alerted Trump about the potential scandal, Trump told him to "get it done." And Cohen did exactly that.

For help, Cohen went to Trump Organization CFO Allen Weisselberg, a longtime employee familiar with organization finances (also a trustee of the trust set up by Trump in 2017 before he became president). The man in control of the Trump Organization's money trail, Weisselberg was a valuable witness for prosecutors. A keeper of the books and financial secrets, Weisselberg was granted immunity in exchange for his cooperation, including testifying before a grand jury in Cohen's Southern District of New York case, as well as providing financial information related to the hush money payments and reimbursements issued by the Trump Organization to Cohen.

Federal prosecutors offer full or partial immunity to an individual who they believe has valuable information related to a pending investigation or prosecution even though the individual may have participated in criminal activity. When the testimony of one witness is so valuable, justice merits the granting of immunity and a promise of no prosecution as fair trade for the full cooperation and testimony of the witness. A non-prosecution deal is a formal agreement between the witness and prosecutors setting forth their respective obligations, namely, that the witness shall cooperate fully and truthfully and not engage in any further criminal activity, and in exchange for his/her cooperation, the prosecution promises not to indict or bring formal charges against the individual. The agreement also details the scope of immunity being offered as well as parameters and limitations that are applicable given the facts and circumstances of the case. The offer of immunity and non-prosecution to Weisselberg signifies that he was a key witness for the SDNY prosecutors who sought information, financial records, and grand jury testimony from him in their case against Cohen.

Cohen and Trump, along with Weisselberg, had a difficult time settling on a manner of payment to Daniels. In fact, Cohen missed an initial deadline of making the agreed upon $130,000 payment. After Daniels again threatened to come forward, Cohen bit the bullet and made the payment himself. On October 26, 2016, Cohen directed $131,000 from his home equity line (HELOC) to be deposited into his newly organized LLC, Essential Consultants. On bank forms, Cohen noted the purpose of the wire was for a "retainer" fee. The hush agreement Cohen drafted featured aliases: Peggy Peterson for Daniels and David Dennison for Trump (the choice of aliases is interesting as P corresponds to Plaintiff and D stands for Defendant, even though no lawsuits were pending at the time).

Months after Daniels was paid and after Trump had become president, Cohen began submitting monthly invoices for $35,000 to the Trump Organization, which complied by sending eleven reimbursement checks to Cohen totaling $420,000. The Trump Organization accounted for the checks as "legal expenses," when in fact by 2017 Cohen was doing little to no legal work for Trump. Notably some of the checks were personally signed by Trump himself. With Cohen running interference, agreements were executed and hush monies were paid so the damaging stories didn't emerge until long after the election in early 2018. Once again the fixer had done his job and done it well.

The hush money payments weren't the only questionable activities Cohen carried out for the Trump campaign. He also participated in extensive planning and communications surrounding the proposed Trump Tower Moscow project, a potential $1 billion deal. Discussions regarding the Moscow project stretched well into June 2016, the height of Donald Trump's campaign, and included Trump's children, Donald and Ivanka. And Felix Sater, a murky figure with connections to the Trump Organization and the Russian underworld, served as a liaison with the Kremlin. While in a July 26, 2016, tweet Trump claimed he had "ZERO investments in Russia," he had in fact signed a letter of intent in October 2015, and in the following months he discussed traveling to Russia to meet with possible financing partners and government officials. Cohen spent most of the duration of the campaign trying to advance the project, while the fixer continuously briefed Trump on the project's progress into late 2016.

Investigation

Almost as soon as Mueller launched his investigation, the special counsel's focus shifted to Cohen. As the president's fixer and someone with intimate knowledge of events and activities within the Trump orbit, who better than Cohen to provide potentially valuable information in the investigation, at least as it related to Trump and members of his campaign?

In mid-July 2017, the FBI sought and obtained a search warrant for one of Cohen's Gmail accounts, followed by three subsequent search warrants that were obtained in the second half of 2017 related to Cohen's iCloud, additional Gmail accounts, and a separate email account.

On August 28, 2017, as the congressional Russia investigations intensified and focused on people close to Trump and his campaign, Cohen submitted a two-page letter to the Senate Select Committee on Intelligence (SSCI) and the House Permanent Select Committee on Intelligence (HPSCI) about his efforts and involvement in the Trump Tower Moscow project in 2016. Specifically, Cohen deliberately misrepresented the time frame within which communications about the project had taken place, tried to downplay and minimize the number of times he had briefed Trump on the project's progress, denied that he had considered asking Trump to travel to Russia, and lied about the response he received from the Russian government following his outreach efforts. And though involved intimately with the project well into June 2016, Cohen stated that talks for the project had stalled by January 2016.

In closed-door testimony on February 28 and March 6, 2019, before the House Intelligence Committee, Cohen testified that ahead of his 2017 letter to Congress he had extensive discussions with President Trump's personal counsel, Jay Sekulow, who advised him to "stay on message" and not contradict Trump (Sekulow pushed back on Cohen's claims). Cohen understood the importance of adhering to the "party line," promoting the president's false message that he had no financial, business, or personal connections to Russia. For Cohen, following the "party line" meant submitting false statements and giving false testimony to Congress about Trump and Russia. To that end, Cohen states that he talked frequently with Sekulow—at least five conversations on the day prior to submitting his letter to Congress. Cohen's account is corroborated by phone records. He further testified that he did not recall speaking to Trump directly about the specifics of his statement or his testimony, but that they spoke "more generally" about his plans to stay "on message." Cohen added that his "agenda," adhering to the "party line" to protect Trump and minimize his Russia links, led him to submit the false statements and provide false testimony before Congress.

Cohen's lies were deliberate. If conversations about the project had ceased in January 2016, they would have ended before the Iowa caucuses, the official start of the presidential campaign season. Continuing the talks through June meant they were ongoing after Trump clinched the Republican Party's nomination. Trump and Cohen spoke frequently about the project. And Sater and Cohen discussed in May 2016 the possibility of Trump traveling to Russia after becoming the Republican nominee. Cohen, at the guidance of Trump's personal counsel, also failed to include his outreach to Putin's office in 2015 in an attempt to set up a meeting between Putin and Trump, a lie by omission.

The special counsel seized on Cohen's false statements and also saw Cohen as a central figure in Trump's orbit. Having been appointed to investigate Russian interference with the 2016 presidential election and related matters, Mueller had the broad authority to pursue "any matters" that arose from that investigation. Not long after his appointment, Mueller established a pattern of referring out ancillary criminal violations like financial crimes and tax evasion to other branches of the Department of Justice. As for Cohen, except for the false statement charge stemming from Cohen's August 2017 letter and subsequent congressional testimony, Mueller referred prosecution of all of Cohen's criminal violations including the allegations of campaign finance law violations to the U.S. Attorney's Office for the Southern District of New York.

By early 2018, as the SDNY built its case against Cohen, further search warrants were issued for Cohen's emails, phones, and properties. On April 7, 2018, a search warrant was obtained for cellphone location data for two of Cohen's many phones, and the very next day search warrants were issued for properties connected to Cohen: his family's Manhattan home, his office at 30 Rockefeller Plaza, a hotel room where the family had been staying during renovations of their home, and a safety deposit box at a New York bank. FBI agents raided Cohen's properties on April 9, 2018.

The FBI seized 4 million files. A bully and scoundrel, Cohen's conduct was often far from ethical or lawyerly. Nonetheless, he was a licensed attorney in the State of New York. This begged the question: which, if any, of Cohen's files were protected by the attorney-client privilege? This privilege applies to communications between attorneys and their clients. The privilege belongs to the client and is invoked to prevent any other person from disclosing "confidential communications." Not every confidential communication is privileged, however. And as to those that are protected, the privilege may be waived, and exceptions may prevent its application. For example, under the crime-fraud exception, to the extent that an attorney and his client are perpetrating a fraud or furthering or committing a crime, those communications are not privileged.

A legal battle ensued between SDNY prosecutors, Cohen's legal counsel, and the Trump legal team regarding attorney-client privilege and the task of identifying those of the 4 million files that contained materials protected by the privilege. The prosecutors fought for all of the seized files while counsel for Cohen claimed attorney-client privilege prevented the disclosure and production of the files as evidence in the case against Cohen. And President Trump, of course, asserted attorney-client privilege as to any file remotely damaging or disparaging to him, tweeting one day after the raids, "Attorney-client privilege is dead!"

Trump's concern that many of his communications with Cohen would fall outside the parameters of the protection under the attorney-client privilege was valid. On paper, Cohen was Trump's personal attorney for a decade. He got things done using the leverage of his counsel and title. But Cohen was more of a fixer who did Trump's dirty deeds and knew where the bodies were buried. While attorney-client privilege is "alive" and in effect, the law does not recognize a fixer-client privilege.

To determine which if any of the Cohen files fell under the protection of the attorney-client privilege, prosecutors sought to create a "taint team" as they customarily do when documents are seized from a law office or attorney. A taint team consists of prosecutors who are unrelated to the case and who are specially appointed to review files and documents to assess what if any of the fruits of the seizure are protected and undiscoverable evidence under the law. Following litigation and hearings in the Southern District of New York, Judge Kimba Wood agreed to assign the document review to "a special master." In Cohen's case, after a three-month review, special master Barbara Jones determined that only 7,500 of the 4 million seized files—a mere 0.2 percent—were protected by attorney-client privilege. A handful of files were also not released because they were found to be highly personal in nature. Among the files seized in the raid were twelve audio recordings, including the one between Cohen and Trump discussing the payment to McDougal that was later reported by CNN's Chris Cuomo.

In the weeks following the raid, Trump began to express concern that Cohen would flip on him, giving rise to a pattern of praise by the president who called his longtime fixer "a fine person with a wonderful family" and the searches "a real disgrace." Some of that messaging was courtesy of Cohen's lawyer, Robert Costello, who was in talks with Trump lawyer Rudy Giuliani. "You are 'loved' . . . they are in our corner . . . Sleep well tonight, you have friends in high places," Costello wrote to Cohen in April 2018, a hint that he would be pardoned if he protected Trump. Trump also called Cohen directly, telling Cohen to "hang in there" and "stay strong." And in the months after the raid, the Trump Organization continued to pay Cohen's legal fees.

Trump's compliments regarding Cohen were short-lived. Trump demonstrated a blatant praise-to-castigation pattern when it came to Cohen. While after Cohen's arrest Trump expressed sadness about his personal attorney's plight, as soon as signs emerged pointing to Cohen cooperating with investigators, such as hiring former Clinton lawyer Lanny Davis in the summer of 2018, Trump turned on Cohen, calling him a rat, a liar, a weak person, and a bad lawyer. Later he even suggested that Cohen's father-in-law should be investigated for criminal activity. Shortly after Special Counsel Robert Mueller filed his December 7, 2018, sentencing memorandum, Trump again tweeted about Cohen, writing that his fixer's conduct was "TERRIBLE, unrelated to Trump. . . . He makes up stories to get a GREAT & ALREADY reduced deal for himself, *and gets his wife and father-in-law (who has the money?) off Scott Free.* He lied for this outcome and should, in my opinion, serve a full and complete sentence."

Crime and Cooperation

Southern District of New York

On August 22, 2018, Cohen pleaded guilty to eight counts: five violations of Title 26 U.S.C. § 7201 (tax evasion), one violation of Title 18 U.S.C. § 1014 (false statements to a financial institution), one violation of Title 52 U.S.C. § 30118(a) and Title 52 U.S.C. § 30109(d)(1)(A), one violation of Title 18 U.S.C. § 2(b) (unlawful campaign contributions), one violation of Title 52 U.S.C. § 30116(a)(1)(A), Title 52 U.S.C. § 30116(a)(7) and

Title 52 U.S.C. § 30109(d)(l)(A), and Title 18 U.S.C. § 2(b) (excessive campaign contribution).

A conviction under 26 U.S.C. § 7201 requires proof beyond a reasonable doubt that the defendant willfully attempted to evade any taxes or payment of the taxes under the Internal Revenue Code statutes incorporated in Title 26 of the U.S. Code. Section 7201 prohibits tax evasion, and the element of willfulness relates to the defendant's intent, meaning that the defendant acted deliberately in the failure to report income or pay taxes. Cohen pleaded guilty to the five violations of Section 7201 because between 2012 and 2016 he failed to report more than $4 million in income to the IRS, including more than $2.4 million received from personal loans connected to his Chicago taxi medallions. He also hid income and sources of income from his accountant and the IRS, including $200,000 in consulting income from an assisted living company and $30,000 from the sale of a rare French handbag. Cohen's consistent pattern of failing to report income and failing to pay taxes on income from multiple sources for consecutive years establishes that this was by no means an oversight or benign omission. Rather, he acted deliberately with the intent to defraud the United States of income tax monies he owed. Having willfully failed to report income and pay taxes on income for at least five years, Cohen was in clear violation of Section 7201.

Title 18 U.S.C. § 1014 is violated when the defendant "knowingly" makes "a false statement or report, or willfully overvalued any . . . property or security, for the purpose of influencing in any way the action of . . . any institution the accounts of which are insured by the Federal Deposit Insurance Corporation." Cohen's guilty plea to this violation was also well supported by the evidence. Between 2010 and 2016 Cohen misrepresented and omitted information from financial statements and other disclosures that he submitted to banks in an effort to absolve a $22 million debt he owed on loans for his taxi medallions (medallions are required to operate taxis in New York City). The loans were issued to LLCs controlled by Cohen and his wife, Laura, both of whom provided personal guarantees to secure the loans. After the taxi medallions lost value due to the popularity of ride-sharing apps, Cohen eventually stopped making payments on the loans, claiming poverty while raking in millions in consulting payments that he did not report. Additionally, in a December 2015 application for a home equity line of credit with First Republic Bank, Cohen made false statements about his net worth and monthly expenses, including failing to disclose more than $20 million he owed to another bank. As a result, the Cohens were later approved for a $500,000 line of credit. Cohen accepted responsibility and pleaded guilty to this charge as the investigation uncovered an abundance of financial evidence that demonstrated that Cohen would regularly submit false and fraudulent information to financial institutions, overstating his assets or understating his liabilities as it suited his financial needs.

The long list of counts to which Cohen pleaded guilty also included violations of Title 52 U.S.C. §§ 30118(a), 30109(d)(1)(A), 30116(a)(1)(A), and 30116(a)(7), commonly known as campaign finance law violations. And Cohen accepted responsibility for these violations as a principal under the aider and abettor law, Title 18 U.S.C. § 2(b). Free and transparent elections are a cornerstone of our democracy, and campaign finance violations erode faith in the electoral process and severely compromise our election and voting laws. Prosecuting such crimes is a priority, and the Cohen-Trump conspiracy to commit campaign finance violations was presented as an open-and-shut case.

Title 52 of the federal code regulates voting and elections, and Section 30118(a) prohibits contributions and expenditures by specific entities including corporations and national banks related to a primary election or in connection with a presidential election. Section 30109(d)(1)(A) of the law defines liability for unlawful campaign contributions based on dollar amount. An individual who "knowingly and willfully" makes or receives a contribution, donation, or expenditure related to a primary election where the total amount exceeds $25,000 in one calendar year violates Section 30109(d)(1)(A). Section 30116 subsections (a)

(1)(A) and (a)(7) of Title 52 further regulate campaign contributions and expenditures. Subsection (a)(1)(A) prohibits "contributions to any candidate . . . with respect to any election for Federal office which, in the aggregate, exceeds $2,000." And subsection (a)(7) goes further to define contributions to a candidate: "expenditures made by any person in cooperation, consultation . . . with or at the request or suggestion of a candidate . . . shall be considered a contribution to such candidate."

The payments to McDougal and Daniels were both illegal campaign expenditures and contributions in violation of Title 52. And as to both payments, Cohen acted at the direction of Individual-1, Donald Trump. While Trump claimed the payments were personal, not political, and not meant to influence the campaign, there is overwhelming evidence proving otherwise. As part of its immunity agreement, AMI corroborated Cohen's account of the transaction by admitting that the $150,000 payment to McDougal was in concert with a candidate's presidential campaign and that its principal purpose was in fact to suppress McDougal's story and to prevent her from influencing the election.

While Trump has called Cohen a liar and tried to discredit his former attorney, the evidence isn't limited to Cohen's words. Cohen's account has been substantially corroborated by others including AMI, David Pecker, and Allen Weisselberg, as well as by financial documentation, namely, copies of the eleven reimbursement checks issued by the Trump Organization for Cohen's advance of the $130,000 hush money payment to Stormy Daniels. And even stronger corroboration is one that involves audio evidence: the damning recording of Cohen's conversation with Trump not only establishes Trump's knowledge of the payment of the McDougal hush money but also demonstrates his central role in its orchestration.

Cohen's orchestration of the $150,000 payment by AMI for McDougal's catch and kill scheme violates Sections 30118(a) and 30109(d)(1)(A) of Title 52. In one calendar year, Cohen induced a payment six times the statutory cap of $25,000 to protect a presidential candidate, a campaign expenditure. Specifically, he urged AMI, a corporation, to advance $150,000 to McDougal as part of the sham deal the sole purpose of which was to suppress McDougal's story. Payment of a campaign expenditure by a corporation violates Section 30118(a), and the value of AMI's payment at Cohen's urging further violates Section 30109(d)(1)(A).

The prosecutors in the Southern District of New York also had more than ample evidence to support Cohen's violations of campaign finance laws with respect to Stormy Daniels's $130,000 payment under Title 52 U.S.C. § 30116 subsections (a)(1)(A) and (a)(7), as well as Section 30109(d)(l)(A). The $130,000 payment to Daniels was an illegal campaign expenditure over the $2,000 cap under subsection (a)(1)(A), Also, Cohen acted willfully (with the intent to help candidate Trump avoid negative influence on his campaign and his chances in the 2016 election) when he made a contribution to protect Individual-1, who was a candidate for federal office. Notably, because Cohen made the expenditure "in coordination with and at the direction of" candidate Trump, he was also in violation of Title 52 U.S.C. § 30116(a)(7). And as with the McDougal payment, Cohen's payment to Daniels was also in excess of the $25,000 limit per calendar year under Title 52 U.S.C. § 30109(d)(1)(a).

Cohen engaged in unlawful campaign financing transactions with the sole intention of aiding candidate Trump. Cohen's campaign finance violations were part of his decade-long "fixing" of Trump's quandaries. With Cohen's help, Trump was protecting neither his reputation nor his marriage but rather his presidential campaign against potential harm. And Cohen was the best conduit to carry out the dirty deeds. Both hush money schemes proved to be clumsy cover-ups of blatant violations of campaign finance laws specifically intended to protect candidate Trump in the 2016 election. While the record was replete with evidence of political motive, it was devoid of evidence of a personal motive!

As discussed in the preceding chapters, under Title 18 U.S.C. § 2—the aider and abettor statute under federal law—a defendant is punishable as a principal if he "commits an offense against the United States or

aids, abets, counsels, commands, induces, or procures its commission."
With respect to the illegal and excessive contributions, that is, payoffs
to women for their silence to protect presidential candidate Trump
(violations of Title 52 U.S.C. §§ 30118(a), 30116(a)(1)(A), 30116(a)(7),
and 30109(d)(1)(A)), Cohen committed and procured the commission
of unlawful acts against the interests of the United States, namely,
our elections and democracy. He was punishable as a principal even
though Trump was the sole and direct beneficiary of Cohen's violations
of campaign finance laws.

The charges against Cohen were supported by the evidence, some
of which was also incriminating against his wife, Laura. But while trial
was not a winnable option for Cohen, he was not offered a cooperation
deal in the Southern District of New York. And though Cohen patently
regrets his decade of loyalty to Donald Trump, the decision to enter
into a negotiated plea agreement in the SDNY is not one that Cohen
should ever regret. On August 21, 2018, Cohen entered into a plea deal
with prosecutors in the SDNY. As Laura was a holder of some of the
accounts involved with the illegal schemes, Cohen was justifiably concerned that his wife could face prosecution at least for false statements
to a financial institution: "She's the love of my life. What am I going to
do? You think I'm going to let them bring her into this craziness? Not a
chance," Cohen told Jeffrey Toobin of the *New Yorker* before reporting
to prison in May 2019.

On August 21, 2018, Cohen pleaded guilty to tax evasion, false statements to a financial institution, unlawful campaign contributions, and
excessive campaign contributions because he was in fact guilty of these
offenses. Doing so not only saved Cohen's wife from prosecution but
also helped Cohen avoid a risky trial that could have left him facing
even more years in prison.

Southern District of New York (Special Counsel's Office)
As in Cohen's case involving charges prosecuted by the SDNY, Cohen
pleaded guilty in connection with the charge brought against him by

the Special Counsel's Office. With the abundance of incriminating evidence gathered by the Mueller team, Cohen couldn't cast reasonable doubt in the case against him. The Mueller prosecutors had access to millions of files, many of which refuted Cohen's false statements about the Trump Tower Moscow project efforts. In an effort to protect Trump, Cohen submitted false statements to Congress in an August 2017 letter and subsequently testified falsely during his October 2017 appearances before Congress.

Violations of 18 U.S.C. § 1001 (a)(2) (making false statements) are the common denominator for the men in Trump's orbit who were indicted or convicted. For Cohen to have been found guilty of a violation of 18 U.S.C. § 1001, prosecutors would have to prove beyond a reasonable doubt that he (1) made a false statement in a matter within the jurisdiction of a specific branch of government; (2) acted willfully (deliberately and with knowledge that his statements were not true); and (3) the statements were material to the agency's decisions or activities. Between Cohen's August 28, 2017, letter to his October 24 and 25, 2017, testimony, Cohen made multiple deliberate misrepresentations to Congress: that the Trump Tower Moscow project communications had ceased in January 2016 (fact: they continued well into the summer of 2016), that Cohen "never considered asking" Trump to travel to Russia in connection with the project (fact: Cohen discussed a potential trip to Russian with Trump, and his executive assistant later gave Trump's passport to Cohen as the trip was being considered), that Cohen had only been in contact with Trump three times about the project (fact: Cohen regularly briefed Trump, and Trump would inquire about the project's status), and that Cohen's outreach to Vladimir Putin's press secretary, Dmitry Peskov, didn't draw a response (fact: it resulted in an email response and a phone call with a Kremlin representative).

Cohen pleaded guilty to making false statements after having willfully lied to Congress about his communications and interactions in connection with the Moscow project, his interactions with Trump about the project, as well as his communications with the Kremlin. At the time of his testimony, Cohen knew that his statements were false. Having to do with Cohen's communications surrounding the project, a massive real estate investment in Russia, Cohen's lies were material to the congressional investigation into contacts between Trump, his campaign, and Russian officials regarding the 2016 interference in our election. Perhaps a telltale sign of the significance and materiality of Cohen's lies is that while Mueller sent out Cohen's laundry list of offenses to the Southern District of New York for prosecution, he retained the 1001 violation for prosecution by his own team.

Sentence

Southern District of New York

In the months leading up to his November 2018 guilty plea on the false statements charge, Cohen met with the Special Counsel's Office seven times for a total of seventy hours and provided information that was deemed to be reliable. In fact, Cohen was cited 136 times in the Mueller Report, second only to former White House counsel Don McGahn.

Based on Cohen's offense level under the Federal Sentencing Guidelines and his lack of criminal history, SDNY prosecutors agreed to a guideline range of fifty-one to sixty-three months for his "veritable smorgasbord" of crimes. While taking Cohen's seventy hours of meetings with Special Counsel's Office investigators and additional meetings with the SDNY into consideration in the plea deal, prosecutors wanted to send a clear message that Cohen was neither a victim nor a hero: "Any suggestion by Cohen that his meetings with law enforcement reflect a selfless and unprompted about-face are overstated." On December 12, 2018, Cohen was sentenced to thirty-six months in prison, a term well below the guideline range in his plea agreement.

For a devoted family man like Cohen, a three-year sentence may seem like a lifetime. But all things considered, namely, Cohen's lack of cooperation and any cooperation credits under Section 5K1.1 of the guidelines, a below-guidelines sentence is objectively reasonable.

Cohen's sentence included an order to pay $1.4 million in restitution and a fine of $50,000.

Southern District of New York (Special Counsel's Office)

On December 12, 2018, following a guilty plea to a violation of Title 18 U.S.C. § 1001 (a)(2) (making false statements), Cohen was sentenced to two months in prison (and ordered to pay a $50,000 fine). His sentence in this case runs simultaneously with the thirty-six-month sentence he received in the SDNY sister case.

Although Cohen provided credible information to the Special Counsel's Office and U.S. Attorney's Office for the SDNY, neither office rewarded Cohen by making a formal motion for cooperation credits and a reduction in his sentence. Partial assistance is far from "substantial assistance" under Federal Sentencing Guidelines Section 5K1.1. Cohen "declined to provide full information about the scope of any additional criminal conduct in which he may have engaged or had knowledge." Under the law, cooperation is all or nothing: partial cooperation is the equivalent of no cooperation. It does not amount to "substantial assistance" under Section 5K1.1. Had Cohen cooperated fully and truthfully, he would have had to undergo debriefings about each and every criminal act or scheme he had participated in or had knowledge of, including those unrelated to the charges he was facing. But Cohen refused.

Following his sentencing in both cases, on February 27, 2019, Cohen testified before the House Committee on Oversight and Reform, saying he was "ashamed" of his efforts to "protect and promote" Trump for so many years. He testified, "Donald Trump is a man who ran for office to make his brand great, not to make our country great. He had no desire or intention to lead this nation—only to market himself and to build his wealth and power."

Cohen's testimony was a remarkable turn—a chance for Trump's longtime fixer to restore whatever was left of his credibility and to tell the world the truth about the man for whom he spent a decade doing dirty bidding. As corroboration of his testimony, Cohen provided copies of financial documents, including copies of Trump Organization checks he received as reimbursement for the Stormy Daniels hush money deal.

In the end, Cohen was sent to the big house while "Individual-1" remained in the White House. Shortly before surrendering to federal prison on May 8, 2019, Cohen expressed immense bitterness about his sentence. "I didn't work for the campaign. I worked for him. And how come I'm the one that's going to prison? I'm not the one that slept with a porn star," Cohen told the *New Yorker*. Nonetheless, Cohen has now begun a term of retribution and rehabilitation at Otisville Federal Correctional Institution in New York. Inmate register number 86067-054 will be required to serve 85 percent of his sentence and is expected to be released on December 13, 2021.

CHAPTER 6

ROGER STONE

THE DIRTY TRICKSTER

★ ★ ★ ★ ★

Association: Trump campaign member and informal advisor

Crime: Indicted on five counts of violating Title 18 U.S.C. § 1001(a)(2) and Title 18 U.S.C. § 2 (false statements), one count of violating Title 18 U.S.C. § 1505 and Title 18 U.S.C. § 2 (obstruction of proceeding), and one count of violating Title 18 U.S.C. § 1512(b)(1) (witness tampering)

Sentence: TBD

When others might have felt shame, Roger Stone was proud and defiant.

The longtime political operative was arrested in the early morning hours of January 25, 2019, the latest member of Donald Trump's campaign team to face charges in Special Counsel Robert Mueller's investigation. Immediately upon his release from custody, Stone acknowledged his supporters and extended his arms, posing to mimic his hero, Richard Nixon. It was through Nixon's reelection bid in 1972 that Stone first embraced trickery as a political weapon. More than forty years later, Stone was tangentially connected to another historic political scandal. The braggart, who sports a perpetual tan, crisp shirts, and garish double-breasted suits, has had a colorful career.

Roger Jason Stone Jr. was born August 22, 1952, in Norwalk, Connecticut, and was raised in Lewisboro, New York. He embraced politics at a young age, inspired by reading Barry Goldwater's book *Conscience of a Conservative*. After becoming involved with various local Republican groups and causes throughout his teen years, he decided to attend

George Washington University so he could be closer to the action in Washington DC. By age nineteen, Stone was working as a scheduler on the Committee to Reelect the President, carrying out dirty tricks for a campaign that would shape his DNA. The Nixon tattoo on his back proves that devotion.

National Politics

Roger Stone's ploys during Richard Nixon's 1972 reelection campaign drew the attention of Senate investigators. In one instance, Stone, using the pseudonym of Jason Rainer, flew to Louisville to train an operative to infiltrate and track Democratic organizations. Stone would then pass the information he received to campaign aide Bart Porter. In another, Stone traveled to New Hampshire to contribute to anti-Vietnam Republican Pete McCloskey's campaign from the Young Socialist Alliance, and after receiving a receipt from a campaign worker showing the contribution from the communist group, Stone and Porter sent a letter to the *Manchester Union Leader* attempting to undermine McCloskey's campaign in the Granite State.

These episodes were documented by the Senate Watergate Committee, which studied the Nixon campaign's illicit activities. When Stone's dirty tricks came to light, he left his job as a junior staffer for Senator Bob Dole, but the scandal didn't derail his career. He became the national youth director for Citizens for Reagan in 1976 before becoming president of the Young Republicans in 1977 with the help of lobbyist and lawyer Paul Manafort. In 1980 Stone served as Ronald Reagan's eastern region campaign director, helping Reagan secure New York on his way to victory.

In 1980 Stone and Manafort began their influential lobbying and political consulting firm Black, Manafort, Stone and Kelly. Stone focused on consulting political candidates such as New York City mayor Ed Koch in 1981, New Jersey governor Thomas Kean in 1981 and 1985, and Jack Kemp, the former NFL player turned politician who was elected to the House of Representatives in 1986 and later ran for president. By the mid-1990s, while running Bob Dole's presidential campaign, Stone found himself in the hot seat after the *National Enquirer* revealed he and his wife had placed advertisements in a magazine looking for group sex partners, so the dirty trickster's dirty side wasn't limited to politics. Stone has also been credited for organizing rallies in Miami with the help of his wife, Nydia, during the Florida recount of 2000. He has continued operating on the political fringes, writing his musings on the blog The Stone Zone, making cable TV appearances, and supplying soundbites on candidates of all stripes, including Donald Trump.

Involvement with the Trump Campaign

Stone first became an advisor for Trump during the late 1980s, as the Manhattan real estate developer first considered a political run. Hot off of his ghostwritten best seller *The Art of the Deal*, Trump was being considered as a possible New York gubernatorial candidate to race against Mario Cuomo and a vice presidential possibility in 1988 on George H. W. Bush's ticket. Trump and his then-girlfriend, Marla Maples, attended Stone's 1991 wedding, and Stone served as an advisor as Trump flirted with the possibility of a Reform Party run for president in 1999 and early 2000. Stone also worked with Trump to prevent gambling expansion in New York in the late 1990s. Their support for each other waxed and waned through the years, most notably after Stone tried to ensnare New York governor Eliot Spitzer in a prostitution scandal in 2007 and left a threatening phone message for Spitzer's eighty-three-year-old father, a scandal that infuriated Trump. Stone served as Trump's consultant for roughly six months in 2015 when Trump announced his candidacy for president. But in July 2015, weeks after Trump threw his hat into the ring, Stone departed the campaign. While Trump claims he had fired his advisor, Stone maintains he quit. In an email to his supporters, Stone likened Trump's "Make America Great Again" slogan to Reagan-era messaging, but explained that he couldn't support the campaign's direction. "Unfortunately, the current controversies involving personalities and provocative media fights have reached such a high volume that it has distracted attention from your platform and overwhelmed your core message," Stone wrote. "With this current direction of the candidacy, I no longer can remain involved in your campaign." But despite having left the campaign in an official capacity, Stone remained loyal to Team Trump, serving as an advocate and unofficial advisor to Trump and maintaining contact with campaign employees.

In the spring of 2016, Russian hackers obtained emails from Hillary Clinton's campaign, the Democratic Congressional Campaign Committee, and the Democratic National Committee. They carried out the hacking scheme through phishing and by way of connections to the groups' networks, installing malware, then sending email data to servers leased by the GRU, Russia's intelligence agency.

The hacked emails were first released through a group identified as DCLeaks.com in June 2016, and later when the DNC announced it had been hacked, a so-called lone Romanian hacker known as Guccifer 2.0 emerged online claiming to be behind the hack. Guccifer 2.0 and DCLeaks.com were, in fact, a front for Russian-connected operatives, a cover story meant to draw attention away from Russia's role in hacking the documents.

Eventually the hacked emails were turned over to WikiLeaks, which began releasing them on July 22, 2016. According to Michael Cohen, Trump knew about a forthcoming WikiLeaks dump because Stone called and informed him directly a few days earlier. Cohen addressed the phone call in his February 27, 2019, testimony before the House Committee on Oversight and Reform, testifying that he was in Trump's office when Stone called and that Trump put Stone on speaker phone. Stone said he had just gotten off the phone with Julius Assange and that "within a few days, there would be a massive dump of emails that would damage Hillary Clinton's campaign," Cohen wrote in his prepared statement. "Mr. Trump responded by stating to the effect of 'wouldn't that be great?'" The phone call about WikiLeaks was far from Stone's only contact with Trump during the campaign. Stone and Trump had many mysterious conversations that would become an aspect of Mueller's investigation.

On July 22, 2016, the day WikiLeaks released its first batch of stolen emails, an unidentified senior Trump campaign employee "was directed to contact Stone about any additional releases and whatever damaging information [WikiLeaks] had regarding the Clinton campaign," as alleged in Stone's January 2019 indictment.

For Stone, the hacked emails were a great opportunity to embarrass Trump's opponent—dirty tricks on a global scale. "I have some news for Hillary and Democrats—I think I've got the real culprit. It doesn't seem to be the Russians that hacked the DNC, but instead a hacker who goes by the name of Guccifer 2.0," Stone wrote in an article for Breitbart News on August 5, 2016. In the weeks after the article was published, Stone and the Russian-connected operatives identifying as Guccifer 2.0 began exchanging direct messages on Twitter. In one, Stone wrote he was "delighted" that Twitter had restored Guccifer 2.0's account. These messages coincided with Stone's public and private claims that he had directly or indirectly communicated with WikiLeaks about the stolen Clinton and DNC emails. During this time, Stone was also in touch with two media personalities with closer connections to WikiLeaks: Jerome Corsi, a conspiracy theorist, and radio host Randy Credico.

By late August Stone began teasing a possible "October surprise" to undermine Clinton's election chances. In one tweet, on August 21, 2016, he wrote, "Trust me, it will soon [be] Podesta's time in the barrel," alluding to campaign chair John Podesta, whose hacked emails would be leaked months later. On October 1, 2016, Stone again hinted at an impending email release. "Wednesday @HillaryClinton is done. #WikiLeaks," he wrote on Twitter.

Stone's prediction was only off by a few days. Assange held a teleconference from the Ecuadoran embassy in London on October 4, 2016, but didn't offer any new details on forthcoming email releases. Trump campaign chairman Steve Bannon then reached out to Stone, wondering why Assange hadn't provided more details in the press conference. Assange was worried about his safety, but more emails were coming, Stone confirmed. "A load every week going forward," he wrote. As Stone predicted, WikiLeaks eventually released tens of thousands of emails connected to Clinton and Democratic efforts.

Stone vehemently maintains that he had no direct knowledge about the WikiLeaks dumps and that he only relied on information that was publicly available and on tips from his sources. But many of his statements to investigators about the hacked emails would turn out to be grossly inaccurate, greatly expanding his criminal exposure.

Investigation

The hacks and email releases drew intense focus from the FBI and Congress where the U.S. House of Representatives Permanent Select Committee on Intelligence (HPSCI) and the U.S. Senate Select Committee on Intelligence were tasked in 2017 with investigating Russian interference in the 2016 elections, as well as ties between members of Trump's campaign and Russian officials.

Both the Stone investigation and the hacking case—*United States v. Netyksho et al.*, in which Mueller returned a symbolic indictment against twelve Russian nationals—grew from common search warrants, according to Mueller in a February 15, 2019, response to an objection filed by Stone's legal team. Stone's communications with the operatives posing as Guccifer 2.0 became a major cause for concern, and Stone's public statements about WikiLeaks made him an early focus for investigators.

In May 2017 the HPSCI sent a letter to Stone requesting that he voluntarily appear before the committee and produce any records, documents, emails, and other communication that could aid the investigation. In response, Stone sent a letter stating he had no documents and no emails related to WikiLeaks. Stone testified before the House Intelligence Committee on September 26, 2017, stating under oath that Russia's role in the hacking of the DNC and Clinton campaign chairman Podesta was "yet unproven." When asked directly if he had no emails, texts, or documents related to WikiLeaks, he responded "That is correct. Not to my knowledge."

On January 24, 2019, Mueller filed a sealed indictment against Stone in the District Court for the District of Columbia. Before dawn the following morning, dozens of FBI agents clad in body armor surrounded Stone's Fort Lauderdale home, guns drawn and flashlights illuminating the darkness. The arrest stood in stark contrast to the behind-the-scenes surrenders of preceding suspects, who civilly arranged to turn themselves in through their lawyers. Stone's neighbors watched the arrest, which resembled the takedown of a drug kingpin. Stone recalled to Infowars how he "opened the door to pointed automatic weapons" and claimed the agents "terrorized" his wife and dogs. President Trump called the arrest "very unusual."

Crime and Cooperation

In an indictment filed on January 24, 2019, Stone was charged with seven violations: five counts under Title 18 U.S.C. § 1001(a)(2) and Title 18 U.S.C. § 2 (false statements), one count under Title 18 U.S.C. § 1505 and Title 18 U.S.C. § 2 (obstruction of proceeding), and one count under Title 18 U.S.C. § 1512(b)(1) (witness tampering).

Like many of his predecessors who were indicted in the Mueller investigation, Stone's culpability under Title 18 of U.S.C. § 1001 (making false statements) requires proof beyond a reasonable doubt that he did the following: made a false statement in a matter within the jurisdiction of a specific branch of government; acted willfully (meaning deliberately and with knowledge that his statements were not true); and that the statements were material to the agency's decisions or activities.

The five counts of making false statements are based on five instances in which Stone lied before the House Intelligence Committee on September 26, 2017. In his sworn testimony, Stone told members of the HPSCI that he did not have any emails relating to Julian Assange or any documents, emails, or text messages that refer to Assange; that his WikiLeaks communications only involved Randy Credico; that he did not ask conspiracy theorist and right-wing media figure Jerome Corsi to pass on messages to Assange or to do anything on Stone's behalf; that Corsi hadn't communicated with him via text or email about WikiLeaks; and that he had never discussed his conversations with Corsi with anyone involved in the Trump campaign. The falsehoods uttered by Stone were material because they were directly related to the independent investigation of Russian interference with the 2016 elections and communications with Russian officials by a House committee, a branch of the U.S. government. Stone's falsehoods were willful, as he not only knew that his statements were false but he testified falsely with the intent to mislead the members about his contacts with Assange, Credico, and Corsi, as well as the documents in his possession and control.

For the violation of obstruction of proceeding under Title 18 U.S.C. § 1505, prosecutors would have to prove beyond a reasonable doubt that Stone "corruptly, or by threats or force, or by any threatening letter or communication has . . . obstructed, or . . . endeavored to obstruct the due and proper administration of the law under which any pending proceeding is being had before any department or agency of the United States, or the due and proper exercise of the power of inquiry under which any inquiry or investigation is being had by either the House, or any committee of either the House or any joint committee of the Congress."

The Section 1505 violation in the indictment is supported by Stone's jarring threats against Credico. On April 9, 2018, Stone wrote an email to Credico: "You are a rat. A stoolie. You backstab your friends, run your mouth, my lawyers are dying Rip you to shreds." He also said he would "take that dog away from you," referring to Credico's therapy dog, Bianca. Stone added, "I am so ready. Let's get it on. Prepare to die [expletive]."

On May 21, 2018, Credico wrote to Stone, "You should have just been honest with the house Intel committee. . . . You've opened yourself up to perjury charges like an idiot," to which Stone responded, "You are so full of [expletive]. You got nothing. Keep running your mouth and

I'll file a bar complaint against your friend." Stone also told Credico to take inspiration from the movie *The Godfather: Part II* and do a "Frank Pentangeli" before the HPSCI in order to avoid contradicting Stone's testimony. For those unfamiliar with the movie or in need of a reminder, Frankie "Five Angels" Pentangeli agrees to testify at a Senate hearing and gives a statement to investigators implicating Michael Corleone, but he has a last-minute change of heart and claims the Corleone family is innocent, perjuring himself. Pentangeli later kills himself in custody, taking his secrets to the grave. Stone's conduct is a clear violation of Section 15015: his messages to Credico were threatening and specifically intended to obstruct the proceedings before the House committee.

As to Stone's violations of Title 18 U.S.C. § 1001(a)(2) (false statements) and Title 18 U.S.C. § 1505 (obstruction of proceeding), he was also alleged to be a "principal." Under Title 18 U.S.C. § 2, the aider and abettor statute under federal law, a defendant is punishable as a principal if he "commits an offense against the United States or aids, abets, counsels, commands, induces, or procures its commission." For Stone this means that if he is found guilty by a jury or if he pleads guilty to either or both Sections 1001(a)(2) and 1505 in any of the counts of the January 24, 2019, indictment, he would in fact be guilty of committing multiple offenses: making false statements to members of Congress on September 26, 2017, and obstructing the proceeding: a hearing before the House Intelligence Committee investigating Russian interference with the 2016 elections, both crimes against the interests of the United States. Having committed these offenses himself, he most certainly is considered and would be punished as a principal.

The final count of the indictment charges Stone with a violation of Title 18, U.S.C. § 1512(b)(1) (obstruction of justice by witness tampering). As previously discussed, "whoever knowingly . . . corruptly persuades another person, or attempts to do so, or engages in misleading conduct toward another person, with intent to influence, delay, or prevent the testimony of any person in an official proceeding" is guilty of witness tampering, a form of obstruction of justice.

Much like his former lobbying partner Paul Manafort, Stone was reaching out to a witness in an effort to prevent him from contradicting Stone's statements to the House committee. On October 19, 2017, Stone sent Credico an excerpt of his letter to the HPSCI that identified Credico as his "intermediary" to WikiLeaks, and he urged Credico, if asked by the committee, to falsely match his testimony, specifically that Credico's info had been the basis for Stone's August 2016 statements about contacts with WikiLeaks. Credico was asked in November 2017 to testify before the HPSCI, after which he "spoke and texted repeatedly with Stone." In one text message on November 19, 2017, Stone urged Credico to "stonewall it. Plead the fifth. Anything to save the plan ..... Richard Nixon." At Stone's trial, Credico would be one of the many witnesses called to testify against him. And the damning text messages will be yet more compelling evidence that supports Stone's guilt.

While Stone made numerous efforts to influence or thwart Credico's testimony before the HPSCI, his threatening communications not only satisfy the elements of Section 1505 (obstruction of a proceeding before a House committee through use of threat), but they also support the broader prohibition against witness tampering under Section 1512.

Stone's indictment was a shocking revelation of detailed coordination between Stone and the Trump campaign in pushing for the release of the hacked Clinton and DNC emails, and it also shows direct communication between Stone—someone with close personal ties to Trump—and the Russian-affiliated hackers who attempted to undermine the 2016 elections. President Trump has long claimed that there was "no collusion" between his campaign and Russia, but Stone's efforts severely undermine that position.

Stone struggled to stay quiet following his arrest. He participated in numerous interviews and posted about the case on his social media accounts. On February 15, 2019, District of Columbia Judge Amy Berman Jackson issued a gag order, barring him from commenting publicly. But not even the gag order would keep Stone silent. Following the order, Stone posted an image to his Instagram page, "Who Framed

Roger Stone?" with information about a new version of his book, *The Myth of Russian Collusion: The Inside Story of How Trump Really Won*. His lawyers apologized, but he still wouldn't stop: on February 18, 2019, Stone posted an image of Judge Berman Jackson featuring what appeared to be a rifle scope's crosshairs. Later submitting a formal apology to Berman Jackson, Stone called the post "improper." Following the post, the judge broadened the gag order against Stone, barring him from posting to social media or making any public comments about the charges against him. "I'm not giving you another chance," Berman Jackson told him during a February 21, 2019, court hearing. For the flamboyant trickster, silence might be the most damning sentence of all.

Sentence

Every preceding defendant in the Mueller investigation has been sentenced to time behind bars, even if the sentence is symbolic in length. The question isn't whether Stone will be sentenced to prison. Rather, it's how long he will spend behind bars.

The statutory maximum for each violation of Title 18 U.S.C. § 1001 is five years. If guilty of all five counts in the indictment, Stone faces a maximum sentence of twenty-five years for this violation alone. Likewise, a violation of Title 18 U.S.C. § 1505 carries a five-year maximum sentence. In terms of the statutory maximum sentences corresponding to the charges against Stone, the most serious count in the indictment is Stone's alleged witness tampering under Title 18 U.S.C. § 1512(b)(1), which carries a maximum of twenty years. Stone's maximum exposure if convicted of all charges is fifty years in prison, a term Stone is unlikely to face. Rather, under federal sentencing rules Stone's sentence will be calculated toward an offense level and sentencing range. Other factors that will determine Stone's sentence include the nature and scope of the offense(s), Stone's individual characteristics under Title 18 U.S.C. § 3553 (for example, his age, any health or mental health issues), the need to impose a sentence that reflects retribution, deterrence, incapacitation, and rehabilitation; the types of sentences available, and the need to avoid unwarranted sentencing disparities among defendants under similar circumstances (in Stone's case, the judge could consider sentences issued thus far for similar violations such as for Manafort's).

While the dirty trickster has shown an uncanny knack for self-preservation throughout his career, Mueller has most definitely cornered him like never before, placing Stone himself in the crosshairs of justice.

CHAPTER 7

PARDON ME, PARDON WHO?

ABUSE OF THE PARDON POWER

★ ★ ★ ★ ★

It is unprecedented that so many members of one presidential campaign have been indicted or convicted of not only a wide range of crimes but specifically for making false statements to cover up contacts with a foreign adversary, the very subject of the Mueller investigation, in an effort to protect the president and his campaign. Donald Trump repeatedly claimed that he would surround himself with the "best people" if elected. Beyond typical political corruption, many of Trump's "best people" have engaged in criminal activity and lied in violation of federal law about contacts with Russia.

Instead of distancing himself from his aides and associates who have come under Robert Mueller's scrutiny, Trump has praised and supported many of them both publicly and privately. He continues to attack the investigation, calling it a hoax, a sham, and a witch hunt, sending messages to his implicated aides and associates that he has their backs. Trump has blatantly discouraged them from cooperating with investigators including by sending messages personally and through his lawyers that loyalty will be rewarded. Trump's pardon power gives him broad authority to set aside convictions for crimes against the United States, and he has exercised this power ten times in the first twenty-eight months of his presidency. But which, if any, of the president's aides and associates could be in line for a presidential pardon?

Whereas previous presidents have generally consulted with the Justice Department or have followed a strategic process when issuing pardons, with many waiting until the end of their terms to issue more controversial pardons, Trump has flouted those conventions by sending loud and clear messages with his issued pardons—not only to his supporters and critics but specifically to his aides and associates being investigated in the Mueller probe.

Under Article II, Section 2, Clause 1 of the U.S. Constitution, the president has the authority to completely set aside or commute (lessen) the punishment for a federal crime. While most pardons are submitted to the president through the Office of the Pardon Attorney for the Justice Department, which considers applications only from individuals who have served their sentences, presidents can bypass that process. And the pardon power may in fact be exercised after the commission of a crime, either before indictment and prosecution, while charges are impending, or after conviction and judgment (sentencing). So bottom line, a president can grant a pardon at any time after the commission of the crime. And while the president's power to pardon is broad in terms of who, why, and when, the authority is not unfettered as to "what": a president can only pardon offenses "against the United States," meaning federal, not state, crimes. With the exception of offenses subject to impeachment, most federal crimes qualify for pardoning.

It is not unusual for a president to exercise his pardon power for violations of federal law. In fact, the practice dates back to George Washington's presidency. Confederate soldiers, anarchists, killers, polygamists, and bootleggers have all been pardoned. Even a former president, Richard Nixon, was granted a full and unconditional pardon by Gerald Ford in 1974. Bill Clinton issued a pardon for his brother as well as international fugitive Marc Rich after Rich's ex-wife donated $450,000 for the Clinton presidential library. George H. W. Bush pardoned advisors to his predecessor, Ronald Reagan, including former secretary of defense Caspar Weinberger, for their roles in the Iran-Contra scandal.

Although undoubtedly presidents have broad authority to issue pardons as they see fit, a pardon by President Trump of any of his former aides and associates indicted or convicted in the Mueller investigation would mark an unprecedented event that further exposes the president for obstruction of justice. Even his attorney general, William Barr, admitted during his January 2019 confirmation hearing before the Senate Judiciary Committee that it would "be a crime" for a president to reward an individual's silence on their behalf with a pardon. But that hasn't stopped Trump from his pattern of praising as a prelude to pardons—both privately and publicly, himself and through his legal team—for his former associates who've been indicted, the majority of whom were also convicted.

Trump's deputy campaign chairman, Rick Gates, and foreign policy advisor George Papadopoulos, who Trump nicknamed "coffee boy" in an effort to downplay his contributions to the campaign, haven't registered on Trump's pardon priority list, presumably either because they were never particularly close to him, don't have a long history of loyalty or support, or both.

Among the six associates charged in Mueller's investigation, Manafort, Flynn, and Stone have maintained Trump's respect and are more likely candidates for pardons. Trump has suggested in more ways than one that Manafort's loyalty would be rewarded. The president has said that a pardon for Manafort was possible while publicly and privately discouraging him from cooperating with investigators (privately Trump expressed concern about what Manafort might know that might be harmful to him). On June 15, 2018, when Manafort's bail was revoked, Trump tweeted that the situation was "very unfair." Just two days later, Trump's personal lawyer, Rudy Giuliani, said Trump and his advisors would consider pardons for people who had been "treated unfairly." Giuliani opened up further in other interviews, saying he and Trump discussed the potential repercussions if Trump decided to pardon Manafort and that when the Mueller investigation is complete, "things might get cleaned up with some presidential pardons."

On August 22, 2018, following Manafort's conviction after the trial in the Eastern District of Virginia, the president was asked about pardons. He sidestepped the question: "I have great respect for what he's done in terms of what he's gone through." It's clear, based on Trump's conduct toward Manafort, that his praise and support were directly responsive to Manafort's loyalty and silence, two features that make the former lobbyist worthy of a pardon for Trump. It's appalling that a president and his lawyer would publicly contemplate a pardon for someone who was silenced in part through obstructive conduct, but these are unprecedented times.

In stark contrast to Manafort, Michael Cohen became the subject of Trump's vitriol. After Cohen's office and residences were raided in April 2018, Trump sent private and public messages of support to Cohen, calling him a "good man" and the search "a real disgrace." Having communicated with Giuliani, Cohen's attorney, Robert Costello, told his client: "You are 'loved' . . . they are in our corner . . . Sleep well tonight, you have friends in high places." This led Cohen to believe he would be "taken care of by the President, either through a pardon or through the investigation being shut down." All Cohen thought he had to do was to stay on "message." But after Cohen pleaded guilty in a cooperation plea agreement on August 21, 2018, stating that he worked "at the direction of Individual-1," Trump, in the hush money scheme ahead of the 2016 election, Trump's goodwill immediately vanished. "I feel very badly for Paul Manafort and his wonderful family," Trump tweeted. "'Justice' took a 12 year old tax case, among other things, applied tremendous pressure on him and, unlike Michael Cohen, he refused to 'break'—make up stories in order to get a 'deal.' Such respect for a brave man!" Trump's clear message: upon cooperating with prosecutors and disengaging from the party line, Cohen was no longer a good man who was deserving of praise. No praise, no pardon.

In the context of pardon worthiness, Flynn represents the biggest unknown of the group. He is someone for whom Trump has expressed great admiration and gratitude even though the three-star general began cooperating with prosecutors and investigators at the time of his December 1, 2017, guilty plea. Following Flynn's resignation after having lied to the FBI and the White House about his communications with Russia, Trump described him as a "wonderful man" and a "fine person," common terms of praise and endearment in Trump language. Trump also passed along messages of support to Flynn through his aides. But after Flynn withdrew from a joint defense agreement, John Dowd, one of Trump's lawyers, left a voicemail for Flynn's counsel suggesting they give Trump's legal team a "heads up . . . just for the sake of protecting all our interests" if Flynn was sharing information with the government that implicated Trump. When Flynn's team reiterated that they could no longer share information, Dowd told them the decision was "a reflection of Flynn's hostility towards the President" and that he planned to inform Trump.

Despite the implied hostility that was communicated, the president continued to praise Flynn for his "incredible record in the military," and he even pushed a false narrative that the "FBI said he wasn't lying, as I understand it." In June 2019, ahead of his continued sentencing, Flynn hired a new lawyer, Sidney Powell, an outspoken critic of the Mueller investigation, prompting a congratulatory tweet from President Trump: "General Michael Flynn, the 33 year war hero who has served with distinction, has not retained a good lawyer, he has retained a GREAT LAWYER, Sidney Powell. Best Wishes and Good Luck to them both!" Retaining Powell only improves Flynn's pardon worthiness given the president's sentiments about his counsel. As Flynn still maintains respect among Republicans for his long, distinguished career, following the conclusion of Robert Mueller's investigation, conservatives such as Senator Rand Paul (R-KY) called on Trump to pardon Flynn, and Representative Matt Gaetz (R-FL) suggested Trump should pardon Manafort and commute Flynn's sentence.

An advisor and friend of Trump's for decades, Stone best meets the Trump criteria for a pardon. The president expressed great remorse over Stone's January 2019 arrest and sought an FBI policy review, saying he was "very disappointed" by how the arrest was handled. During a February 3, 2019, interview with CBS, when asked about

Stone, Trump replied: "Roger is somebody that I've always liked. . . . I have not thought about [a pardon]. It looks like he's defending himself very well. But you have to get rid of the Russia witch hunt." Given his loud and clear statements about pardons, the president's claim that he hasn't thought about a pardon for Stone, paired with the need "to get rid of the Russia witch hunt" and against the backdrop of Giuliani's suggestion that "things might get cleaned up" with pardons at the end of the investigation, Stone remains a very likely candidate for a Trump pardon.

By early 2019, even Papadopoulos was angling for his conviction to be set aside: "My lawyers have applied for a pardon from the president for me. . . . If I'm offered one I would love to accept it, of course." No, really? Some individuals are actually hesitant to accept a pardon due to its optics of guilt, but that isn't a concern for Papadopoulos, whose pardon, if ever granted, would follow a guilty plea and sentence.

Aside from his direct and indirect messages of support to his felonious aides and associates, the ten pardons President Trump issued in his first twenty-eight months in office likewise set the tone for what and who merits the gift of his exercise of the presidential pardon power:

- Joseph M. Arpaio (August 27, 2017)
- Kristian Mark Saucier (March 9, 2018)
- I. Lewis "Scooter" Libby (April 13, 2018)
- Jack Johnson (May 24, 2018)
- Dinesh D'Souza (May 31, 2018)
- Dwight Lincoln Hammond and Steven Dwight Hammond (July 10, 2018)
- Michael Chase Behenna (May 6, 2019)
- Patrick James Nolan and Conrad Moffat Black (May 15, 2019)

Many of President Trump's pardons reflect his self-interests, political rivalries, and legal frustrations. His pardon of Joe Arpaio, a former Arizona sheriff who had been found in contempt of court for violating a judge's order to stop detaining immigrants due to their legal status, was

Trump's way of offering a favor to a friend. Attending various campaign events, Arpaio was a visible presence during Trump's presidential run. The anti-immigration core of Arpaio's case has been an important part of the Trump campaign and administration.

With his April 13, 2018, pardon of I. Lewis "Scooter" Libby, Trump played to his Republican base and highlighted his legal frustrations. Libby was an advisor to Vice President Dick Cheney and was convicted of obstruction of justice, false statements, and perjury for his role in leaking the identity of undercover CIA officer Valerie Plame Wilson, similar to the charges against the Trump aides and associates, and in the case of obstruction of justice, the criminal offense Mueller documented Trump himself committing on numerous instances. Parts of Libby's sentence had been commuted by President George W. Bush, meaning he was spared from serving a thirty-month prison term. A pardon from President Trump was Libby's icing on the cake.

The president's pardon issued to Dinesh D'Souza for a 2014 conviction of campaign contribution fraud fulfilled a number of the president's objectives. One, it showed his indifference to violations of campaign finance laws, something Trump's former fixer Michael Cohen violated at Trump's direction. The D'Souza pardon came in the same month that Cohen's office and homes were raided by the FBI and at a time when Trump was urging Cohen not to "flip." Second, the prosecutor who indicted D'Souza, U.S. Attorney Preet Bharara, was appointed by Barack Obama and fired by President Trump in March 2017, later becoming an outspoken critic of Trump's. Third, D'Souza was known for his conspiracy-fueled theories about Trump critics Hillary Clinton and Barack Obama and trafficked in racist and inflammatory political rhetoric. Even Roger Stone agreed President Trump was sending a message to Mueller with the pardon of D'Souza: "Indict people for crimes that don't pertain to Russian collusion and this is what could happen. . . . The special counsel has awesome powers, as you know, but the president has even more awesome powers," Stone told the *Washington Post*.

The pardons issued to Conrad Black and Patrick Nolan reflect the president's self-interests as well as his disdain for the Mueller investigation. Black, a media mogul and former business partner, had been convicted of fraud and obstruction of justice in 2007. In 2018 Black released a glowing book on Trump, *Donald J. Trump: A President Like No Other*. Nolan, meanwhile, is a Mueller critic who had faced racketeering charges in the 1990s. Nolan became close with Trump's son-in-law, Jared Kushner, as they worked together on prison reform measures.

President Trump's obsession with the pardon power is no secret. In June 2018 he confirmed the White House had "3,000 names" it was considering for pardons, focusing on seeking justice for those who "really have been treated unfairly." Frustrated by the law and its application, the broad power of the presidential pardon appeals to Trump, and he has come to realize that he can pardon just about anyone at any time, including himself.

Though not the first time contemplated, the question of whether a president can legally and ethically pardon himself is unsettled. (Richard Nixon's lawyers considered it during the waning days of his presidency, before his resignation and President Ford issuing a pardon.) Not only does Trump use praise to set the stage for a pardon, but he revels in the pardon power itself: "The pardons are a very positive thing for a President. I think you see the way I'm using them. And yes, I do have an absolute right to pardon myself. But I'll never have to do it because I didn't do anything wrong. And everybody knows it. There's been no collusion. There's been no obstruction. It's all a made-up fantasy. It's a witch hunt. No collusion, no obstruction, no nothing." No president in United States history has ever pardoned himself. But President Trump doesn't see any issues whatsoever with self-pardoning, legal, political, or otherwise.

At the end of the day, the need for Trump to self-pardon was mooted once the Mueller report was released, because by following the Justice Department's Office of Legal Counsel long-established guidance, Mueller could not make a prosecutorial decision regarding President Trump's culpability and indictability. Had Mueller in fact made a prosecutorial determination regarding indictment, or even accused the president of the obstructionist acts he uncovered and detailed in his report, Trump's statements suggest he would undoubtedly pardon himself.

With the need for self-pardon irrelevant, President Trump continues to float suggestions about who he could pardon next, including the aides and associates indicted or convicted in the course of the Mueller investigation. The president drew outrage in May 2019 after he announced he was considering pardons for war criminals who had ruthlessly murdered innocent civilians, an example of Trump's abuse of pardon power and the fact that his pardons themselves are acts of injustice, instead of in response to injustice. Traditionally presidents have used the pardon power to settle injustices, sending messages about an unjust process or an extreme punishment (for example, undue punishment for a nonviolent drug offense). For President Trump, pardons are just a way to reward those who praise or protect him. The message in Trump's pardon is unprecedented: if you support and protect me, you will be pardoned, irrespective of fairness of process and punishment. This abuse of the pardon power is an unprecedented subversion of the justice system.

CHAPTER 8

THE MUELLER REPORT

RUSSIAN INTERFERENCE AND PRESIDENTIAL OBSTRUCTION OF JUSTICE

★ ★ ★ ★ ★

In May 2017 Special Counsel Robert Mueller III, a lifelong lawman who served as FBI director from 2001 to 2013, was appointed to investigate "(i) any links and/or coordination between the Russian government and individuals associated with the campaign of President Donald Trump; (ii) any matters that arose or may arise directly from the investigation; and (iii) any other matters within the scope of 28 C.F.R. § 600.(a)." Initially a counterintelligence inquiry into Russian interference with the 2016 election, the investigation soon metastasized into a criminal probe focused on the conduct of President Trump and his associates. The Mueller Report consists of two parts: volume 1 covers the investigation of conspiracy or coordination by members of the Trump campaign with Russians in their interference with the 2016 presidential election, while volume 2 details the evidence and analysis of President Trump's obstructive behavior from the summer of 2016 through the conclusion of the special counsel's investigation. Most Americans, including the president, didn't read the report in its entirety if at all. Clocking in at 448 pages, the report is a comprehensive read that requires commitment of substantial time and attention. Therefore, what follows is a succinct outline of Mueller's findings along with the author's expert analysis.

The Russia probe began with a leak by a loose-lipped "coffee boy." In May 2016, over drinks with an Australian political figure, Trump's foreign policy advisor George Papadopoulos mentioned that the Russian government was prepared to release Hillary Clinton's hacked emails to benefit the Trump campaign. The suggestion was eye-opening and frightening; while email hacking of presidential candidates is no news, interference by a foreign adversary targeted at one candidate over the other was most definitely unprecedented. After WikiLeaks released some of the stolen emails in late July 2016, the Australian politician reported the activity to the FBI. Subsequently, on July 31, 2016, the FBI opened an investigation into whether the Trump campaign was conspiring or coordinating with Russian officials. The investigation into the president's obstruction of justice arose directly from the FBI investigation. After Mueller's appointment in May 2017, the Special Counsel's Office obtained evidence of the president's interactions with then-FBI director James Comey that justifiably raised concerns. The president attacked and undermined the investigation from its inception. And by the spring of 2018, it became evident to the president that he himself was the subject and potentially a target of the investigation, specifically as to conduct that would constitute obstruction of justice.

At its height, Mueller's team had 19 attorneys working alongside approximately 40 staffers. The Special Counsel's Office estimates 500 witness interviews, including almost 80 who testified before a grand jury, along with 2,800 subpoenas, nearly 500 search-and-seizure warrants, and 300 issued court orders in evidence gathering. The investigation cost more than $25 million and led to 199 criminal counts, 37 indictments (34 individuals and 3 entities), 7 guilty pleas, 1 person convicted at trial, and 10 obstructive acts by the president himself.

Upon conclusion of the special counsel investigation in March 2019, Attorney General William Barr released a four-page summary interpretation of Mueller's report, rejecting Mueller's request for Barr to share the report's introduction and executive summaries. And although Mueller had privately sent a letter to Barr responding that the summary "did not fully capture the context, nature, and substance" of the report, Barr failed to discuss his exchange with Mueller in his April

9, 2019, testimony before the House Appropriations Subcommittee. Subsequently, on April 18, 2019, a redacted version of the full 448-page report was released to Congress and the American people.

It's not uncommon for a sitting president to be investigated for criminal conduct. In fact, with the exception of Barack Obama, many presidents since Richard Nixon have faced an independent criminal investigation ranging from Nixon's Watergate break-in and cover-up to Bill Clinton's lies about a sexual affair. What is unprecedented about the Mueller probe is that it was not limited to election interference efforts by Russia but also included an investigation that unveiled brazen acts of obstruction by a sitting president, Donald J. Trump.

Collusion, Confusion, and Mueller's 3 C's

Mueller's investigation into Russian interference in the 2016 election must be viewed in terms of three C's: collusion, conspiracy, and coordination. Since the inception of the Russia probe, the president, his representatives, and his associates have repeatedly stated "no collusion" and "no obstruction." In the context of the Russia probe, "collusion" is nothing but a political term meant to distract from the true scope and purpose of the investigation and its findings. The crime of collusion is nonexistent in the extensive federal criminal code, which contains more than four thousand crimes: there is no federal crime of collusion. No one is sitting in a prison cell whining to his cellmate that he is innocent of collusion. You will, however, find plenty of crimes that punish individuals for email and computer hacking, election fraud, or violations of campaign finance laws. You will also find an array of laws that prohibit obstruction of justice, as well as the most commonly charged federal crime in cases involving more than one defendant, conspiracy.

The legal definition of collusion is "a deceitful agreement or compact between two or more persons" for an "evil purpose," not a crime. Simply put, collusion means coordination with bad motive: you can have collusion without having a criminal conspiracy, but you can't have a criminal conspiracy without some sort of collusion. Irrespective of the varying definitions of "collusion" among politicians and pundits, the term is a red herring, a deliberate diversion that has been adopted by the president and his tribunes as a cover-up to deflect from their countless close contacts with Russia. While collusion became the political buzzword referring to ties between Russia and Trumpworld, Mueller declined to investigate collusion, as it "is not a specific offense or theory of liability found in the United States Code, nor is it a term of art in federal criminal law." Instead, the special counsel focused on whether anyone involved with the Trump campaign *coordinated* with Russia to carry out a *conspiracy* to influence the 2016 election. And although in his investigation of Russia's two-pronged election interference operation Mueller found insufficient evidence to support charges against any members of the Trump campaign for conspiracy or coordination, he did unveil numerous interactions between campaign members and Russian nationals, contact and activity that could loosely be termed "collusion."

To prove conspiracy, the prosecution must demonstrate beyond a reasonable doubt that two or more individuals formed an agreement and that one of them committed an "overt act" (a step toward completing the crime). Completion (commission) of an underlying crime is not a required element of conspiracy.

In the context of the Mueller investigation, "coordination" refers to any actions the Russian government may have taken to advance Trump's candidacy. If those actions were found to be done in consultation with or involving the Trump campaign, they would be considered "in-kind" contributions in violation of federal campaign finance laws barring foreign contributions.

Of the three C's, Mueller was intent on investigating evidence that supported conspiracy and coordination, not collusion.

The 2016 Russian-American Election

A key takeaway from the Mueller Report appears in chilling simplicity in its second paragraph: "The Russian government interfered in the

2016 presidential election in sweeping and systematic fashion." That interference occurred in two ways: one through pro-Trump social media efforts, and the other involving a document hack-and-release operation by Russian intelligence against Hillary Clinton's campaign and other Democratic organizations.

Mueller's investigation into Russian interference with the 2016 election confirmed that the Internet Research Agency (IRA), a Kremlin-connected troll farm, used social media campaigns to try to inflame political and social unrest in the United States through "information warfare." The IRA received funding from Yevgeniy Prigozhin, a Russian oligarch with ties to Vladimir Putin. The IRA sent employees to the United States in mid-2014, a full year before Trump announced his candidacy, to gather intelligence. By early 2016, the group was carrying out a targeted operation on social media that regularly promoted Trump and criticized Democratic challenger Hillary Clinton, along with posing as grassroots political groups and staging political rallies in the United States. Reportedly 126 million people may have been served content on Facebook related to the IRA. In fact, it was after Facebook shared its findings with authorities that the FBI picked up its investigation into the social media efforts. On Twitter, figures such as Donald Trump Jr., Eric Trump, Kellyanne Conway, Michael Flynn, Sean Hannity, and Roger Stone retweeted or responded to IRA-controlled accounts, which were often disguised as U.S.-based individuals or local political groups. In September 2017 Facebook and other social media companies began publicly reporting that they identified Russian expenditures to fund political and social advertisements.

The hack-and-release operation of the interference was carried out through the Russian government's efforts to hack Democratic email systems and to release the hacked emails as a means of embarrassing Clinton toward a defeat. Russia's military intelligence unit known as GRU carried out the cyberattack, stealing hundreds of thousands of documents belonging to Clinton's campaign, the Democratic Congressional National Committee, and the Democratic National Committee.

In mid-June 2016 the Russian government began releasing the hacked emails through two online personas, DCLeaks and Guccifer 2.0, building interest while teasing future leaks. The hacked emails were seen as a political weapon, a way to attack and damage Clinton's campaign at the most inopportune time. Further emails were released through WikiLeaks, the document disclosure company led by Julian Assange. The Russian intelligence officers who carried out the hacks were charged with conspiracy to violate the federal computer-intrusion statute (Title 18 U.S.C. § 1030) among other federal laws.

Email intrusions of presidential campaigns are not unprecedented. In 2008 China infiltrated accounts connected to presidential candidates Barack Obama and John McCain. In that instance, as soon as the hacking activity appeared on the FBI's radar, they notified the campaigns, which responded by bolstering cybersecurity measures. Likewise, with the hack-and-release operation aimed at the Clinton campaign and the Democratic Party, the FBI should have immediately been notified. Instead, the Trump campaign failed to report the foreign adversary's illegal efforts directed at a presidential election, and both Trump and his campaign were fixated on the continued hack-and-release of emails and documents while enthusiastically encouraging the release of more. In fact, the Trump campaign had been planning "a press strategy, a communications campaign, and messaging" based on WikiLeaks releasing emails. And Roger Stone kept in touch with the campaign and Trump himself, providing regular updates on the WikiLeaks hack-and-release operation. (WikiLeaks released troves of emails beginning on October 7, 2016, not so coincidentally on the same day the *Washington Post* released the embarrassing *Access Hollywood* tape.)

On February 16, 2018, a federal grand jury in Washington DC returned an indictment against thirteen Russian nationals and three entities, including the IRA, for the social media election interference. All defendants were charged with conspiracy to defraud the United States, while three of them were also charged with conspiracy to commit wire fraud and bank fraud and five with aggravated identity theft.

Separately on July 13, 2018, twelve Russian nationals were also indicted in connection to the GRU hacking efforts. Those defendants were likewise all charged with conspiracy to defraud the United States, while three were also charged with conspiracy to commit wire fraud and bank fraud and five were charged with aggravated identity theft. The charges were largely symbolic, as the Russian defendants are unlikely to see the inside of a U.S. courtroom.

The Other C: Contacts Galore with Russians

Despite the insufficiency of evidence that the Trump campaign conspired or coordinated in Russian election interference activities, the Special Counsel's Office uncovered an overwhelming number of contacts between the campaign and the foreign adversary. During the course of the investigation, the president's aides and advisors lied in an effort to cover up their communications and contacts with Russia, protecting not only themselves but also the president. Trump's campaign aides and associates were indicted or convicted of violations of Title 18 U.S.C. § 1001 for lying about emails obtained by Russia (George Papadopoulos), phone calls with Russia (Michael Flynn), business deals with Russia (Michael Cohen), lobbying and contacts related to Russia (Paul Manafort and Rick Gates), and facilitating WikiLeaks dumps of emails hacked by Russia (Roger Stone). Nonetheless, while there was extraordinary evidence of contacts and communications with Russia, this conduct alone did not establish guilt of conspiracy or coordination under the law.

Although the special counsel found "no evidence" of conspiracy or coordination by the Trump campaign, he recognized the existence of additional evidence that may have been suppressed by the president's associates. Many individuals invoked their Fifth Amendment right against self-incrimination. Some information was screened from the special counsel's team, and several targets affiliated with the Trump campaign (including Flynn, Papadopoulos, Cohen, and Manafort) lied and obstructed the investigation by providing incomplete information and failing to cooperate with the special counsel. Still others deleted communications or used encrypted applications that did not provide for long-term data retention, creating gaps in the investigation. "Given these identified gaps, the Office cannot rule out the possibility that the unavailable information would shed additional light on the events described in the report." Simply put, while the unavailable communications may not be relevant to conspiracy or coordination with Russia, they also carry the potential of containing incriminating information that could in fact prove guilt beyond a reasonable doubt. We may never know.

While the Mueller investigation unveiled significant criminal activity by Russian nationals, as well as numerous false statements by members of Trump's campaign and administration about their communications, contacts, and ties with Russian individuals and officials, the president continued to claim that the special counsel's investigation was a "witch hunt" and "a hoax": "no collusion, no obstruction." In his incessant iterations of "no collusion," Trump is correct in that there was no *crime* of collusion, and Mueller therefore did not investigate this nonexistent crime. On the other hand, if the president refers to links and contacts between members of his campaign and Russians, then he has deliberately mischaracterized the truth. His claims are flatly contradicted by the special counsel's findings that the campaign did in fact have numerous links with Russians. "No collusion?" Wrong. And "No obstruction?" Most definitely wrong!

The Obstructionist in Chief

While the truth that a foreign adversary interfered with our election and assaulted our democracy is an astonishing and highly concerning revelation in and of itself, perhaps the most extraordinary finding by the special counsel involves ten acts of obstruction of justice by the president himself. Mueller also outlined President Trump and his campaign's response to Russia's influence during the 2016 presidential race as a backdrop for the activity that followed. That criminal conduct is detailed in the 182-page second volume of the Mueller Report, an indictment in all but the formalities.

The evidence of obstruction by the president is absolutely devastating. President Trump

- Attempted to stop, limit, and redirect the Mueller investigation.
- Attempted to fire the special counsel.
- Enlisted others to create false evidence about his own conduct.
- Attempted to prevent and dissuade witnesses from cooperating in investigations into him and his campaign.

In his analysis of the president's obstructive conduct, the special counsel identified and applied the three elements common to federal obstruction statutes: (1) the obstructive act—an effort to impede justice; (2) the nexus—a connection between the act and a pending or contemplated official proceeding; and (3) corrupt intent—acting "knowingly and dishonestly" or "with an improper motive."

To establish guilt of obstruction, sufficient evidence of all three elements must be proved beyond a reasonable doubt. Of the three elements, corrupt intent often poses a challenge of proof, especially as applied to a sitting president who has sweeping constitutional powers.

The special counsel's assessment of the president's efforts to obstruct justice raised a separation of powers issue that hinged in part on whether a sitting president can commit obstruction in the first place. Or in other words, could a sitting president, with broad and sweeping powers under Article II of the Constitution, be investigated for obstruction, and does the special counsel have the authority to evaluate the president's actions for "corrupt intent" if they can be justified with a neutral pretext? "Yes," Mueller answered emphatically in the report.

The special counsel relied on a 1995 dissent opinion (nonbinding authority) by ultraconservative jurist Antonin Scalia, who defined an act conducted with corrupt intent as one that is "done with an intent to give some advantage *inconsistent with official duty* and the rights of others." Mueller's citation of Justice Scalia's opinion served two purposes. First, it established that under federal criminal law, individuals, including government officials, *can* engage in obstruction when they commit a seemingly lawful act with illicit motive. (For example, if the president purports to exercise his constitutional authority to terminate an unsatisfactory subordinate, but in fact fires the subject to impede an investigation into his campaign. Sound familiar? He may have acted "inconsistent with official duty" and therefore with the necessary corrupt intent to obstruct justice.) Second, by relying on Scalia's wisdom as guidance for his assessment of obstruction by a president and whether the acts were executed with corrupt intent, Mueller preempted inevitable criticism that his report failed to respect separation of powers and the president's ability and freedom to govern. Notably, Scalia was a proponent of the "unitary executive" theory, the president is king theory, which endorses vast powers for the president. Scalia's 1995 opinion not only strengthened Mueller's rationale for his authority to investigate the president's official acts but also preempted criticism and complaints that the special counsel's obstruction inquiry chilled the president's freedom to govern. In Mueller's analysis of corrupt intent as to each and every obstructionist act by President Trump, he carefully identifies and examines acts that were inconsistent with an official duty. Gauging the president's corrupt intent, the special counsel considered Trump's pattern of conduct and the totality of evidence and decided that Trump acted corruptly. Corrupt intent poses challenges of proof as to some, but certainly not all, of the president's obstructive acts when the acts are viewed in isolation. But the "totality of the evidence" in the report is a better reflection of the president's motives. Mueller wrote: "It is important to view the President's pattern of conduct as a whole. That pattern sheds light on the nature of the President's acts and the inferences that can be drawn about his intent."

The president failed to appear before the special counsel for an interview, making it difficult to gauge his intent. Instead, through his lawyers, the president reached an agreement by which he submitted heavily vetted written answers, an extremely rare accommodation for the target of a criminal investigation. The president's answers consisted of "incomplete or imprecise" language, including more than thirty occasions where he claimed he "does not recall" or "remember" or have an "independent recollection" of the information sought. Subsequently, when the special counsel requested an in-person interview to address inconsistencies in the president's written answers, the president declined. And although Mueller did consider issuing a subpoena for the president's testimony, the investigation had made "significant progress," and a subpoena would have led to court battles and a lengthy delay in the issuance of the report.

While some of the president's obstructive acts in isolation would potentially present problems of proof as to corrupt intent, his multiple failed attempts and endeavors to obstruct the investigation are in no way defensible. Federal obstruction statutes are not limited to the substantive obstruction offense; they also apply to attempts and endeavors to obstruct. If an individual has the intent to commit an offense and takes an overt act that constitutes a substantial step toward that goal, he is guilty of the attempt to commit the crime. An "endeavor" to obstruct justice, when carried out with corrupt intent, is also prohibited under federal law. In the president's case, his maligned requests were stymied by his enlisted aides and associates. And although dialogue alone is not enough to prove obstruction of justice, any "concrete and specific" acts can constitute a "substantial step," even if assigned to someone else or never carried out. Much like substantive obstruction, an attempted obstruction is a crime. Failed attempts and endeavors don't lessen the president's criminality in any way, shape, or form.

From Russia with Love: The Campaign's Response to Reports about Russian Support for Trump

As the backdrop for the president's obstruction of justice, the special counsel pointed out the campaign's response to investigation into election interference by Russia:

- On July 27, 2016, Trump publicly called on Russia to find Hillary Clinton's missing emails: "Russia, if you're listening, I hope you're able to find the 30,000 emails that are missing."

- Hacked emails from Clinton's campaign were distributed through WikiLeaks.
- President Trump himself discussed the possibility of upcoming leaks.
- Roger Stone kept the president abreast of the situation, calling Trump's office ahead of a July 22, 2016, email dump. "Oh good, all right," Trump responded.
- Trump minimized his personal risks to Russia on various platforms, tweeting it was "crazy" to suggest he had a connection with Russia and that he had "ZERO investments in Russia."
- President Trump's team maintained connections with Russia, even as the outgoing Obama administration issued sanctions in response to Russia's efforts to influence the election.

The report's relevant facts and analysis as to each of the president's obstructive acts are outlined below. While President Trump could be indicted based on the evidence in the report, an indictment contains allegations of crime and requires proof beyond a reasonable doubt in order to arrive at a conviction. Because the president is not above the law, like any other person accused of crimes, he too is presumed innocent until proven guilty beyond a reasonable doubt. The following analysis therefore also includes the author's own assessment about the likelihood of a conviction based on the evidence, using symbols: a 👍 means evidence exists to prove guilt beyond a reasonable doubt; a 👍 👎 means the evidence might be sufficient to prove guilt beyond a reasonable doubt; and 👎 means a conviction is unlikely as the evidence appears insufficient to prove guilt beyond a reasonable doubt. Irrespective of the strength of evidence unveiled by the special counsel and its sufficiency to support a conviction as to each isolated set of obstructive acts, the president is most definitely indictable for obstruction of justice as to *all* episodes of obstructive conduct. Mueller's deferral to Congress and the process of impeachment does not in any way change that conclusion.

Do go Cut Him a Break: The President's Conduct Concerning the Investigation of Michael Flynn

EVIDENCE

- Remember the phone calls between Flynn and Kislyak after the Obama administration issued sanctions against Russia in December 2016? Yes, those.
- Flynn lied to members of the administration and the FBI about the calls. The night after the DOJ warned the White House that Flynn had discussed sanctions and lied about it, the president had a private dinner with James Comey. At the dinner, Trump asked for Comey's loyalty.
- The president met again with Comey after asking Flynn to resign in February 2017. "I hope you can see your way clear to letting this go, to letting Flynn go."
- Deputy National Security Advisor K. T. McFarland was fired, but after being told she could become the next ambassador to Singapore, she received a request from Chief of Staff Reince Priebus to "draft an internal email that would confirm that the president did not direct Flynn to call the Russian ambassador about sanctions," even though McFarland did not know that to be true. McFarland saw the ambassadorship as a quid pro quo for writing the letter. Priebus told McFarland to forget about writing the letter.
- President Trump had Priebus reach out to Flynn and "let him know that the President still cared about him." Priebus believed the outreach was a means of keeping Flynn from saying anything negative about the president.

OBSTRUCTIVE ACT: Trump's February 14, 2017, conversation with Comey in the Oval Office, when he cleared the room to tell the FBI director alone, "I hope you can see your way clear to letting this go, to letting Flynn go. . . . I hope you can let this go." The president's request was a step toward impeding an investigation. (Comey documented the conversation in his notes and in congressional testimony.) While the president publicly disputed some aspects of the account, he also privately confirmed to aides that he mentioned Flynn during his meeting with Comey. Meanwhile, Comey's recollection of the encounter remained consistent, including in testimony under oath and in meetings with senior FBI officials. Other administration officials have corroborated Comey's version of how he and President Trump wound up alone. After the meeting, Comey alerted FBI leadership, who "agreed to keep the President's statements closely held" so the agents investigating Flynn wouldn't be influenced by the president's request. And Comey asked Sessions to prevent him from ever being alone with the president again. Mueller also considered whether the president's request of Comey to "let Flynn go" could be seen as anything other than a direct order, but he believed the circumstances showed the president's actual intent: to end the FBI's investigation of Flynn. For one, Trump arranged to be alone with Comey and excluded Sessions. Second, as the head of the executive branch, "When [Trump] says that he 'hopes' a subordinate will do something, it is reasonable to expect that the subordinate will do what the President wants." The president asked Comey three times to "let this go," and Comey saw the statements as a directive.

NEXUS TO AN OFFICIAL PROCEEDING: At the time the president made this request, he was well aware that Flynn had lied to the FBI. The president therefore could expect that a grand jury would follow. The president was also well aware that Flynn was facing criminal exposure.

INTENT: The special counsel considered numerous possibilities for the president's motive in seeking an end to the FBI's investigation of Flynn. Mueller identified "some evidence" that President Trump was aware of Flynn's calls with Kislyak soon after they occurred but that evidence was inconclusive. Flynn, following the calls, had been proud to keep Russia from exploding over the sanctions. And if Vladimir Putin was happy, one would reasonably expect Flynn would want the president to know. Trump was pleased that Putin didn't retaliate, calling it a "great move." And notably, he never said that Flynn lied to him about the Kislyak calls. At the same time, Mueller raised the possibility that the president might have believed that making the Flynn situation go away would end the broader Russia investigation, something Trump thought was undermining the legitimacy of his presidency. Mueller also assessed whether the president was motivated by sympathy for Flynn. The president gushed about Flynn in public statements, calling him a good man and having aides reach out to his former national security advisor. But according to members of the Trump orbit, privately the president "had become unhappy" and "frequently irritated with Flynn." In his analysis, the special counsel highlighted the president's means of asking Comey about Flynn—one-on-one in a private setting, in a way that ran counter to the advice he received from White House counsel. And if the president hadn't done anything wrong, why did he later deny his request of Comey or suggest McFarland write an internal email that would have absolved him? Why put so much effort into a cover-up if there's no underlying wrong?

As is common with obstruction charges, the president's corrupt intent regarding his request of Comey poses problems of proof. Having not been able to interview the president or examine him pursuant to a subpoena, the special counsel was left with heavily lawyered written answers that made it difficult to assess the president's intent regarding Flynn. As a result, the Special Counsel's Office was left to fill in gaps as to whether or not the president acted corruptly. Despite the challenge to prove intent, Mueller uncovered sufficient evidence to at least indict Trump on obstruction related to his call to cut Flynn a break.

Seeing Red: The President's Reaction to Public Confirmation of the FBI's Russia Investigation

EVIDENCE

- Jeff Sessions was considering recusal from the Russia investigation due to conflicts of interest. (Sessions was a member of President Trump's campaign and met with Russian officials in 2016.)

The president grew furious, asking Sessions to "unrecuse"—an unprecedented request from a president to an attorney general.

It was known within the administration that Sessions would have to recuse himself regarding any investigations related to the president's campaign.

- On March 2, 2017, White House counsel Don McGahn, at the president's urging, contacted Sessions to tell him Trump was "not happy about the possibility of recusal." Sessions ended up recusing himself despite the criticism.

- The day after Sessions's recusal, the president called McGahn into the Oval Office: "I don't have a lawyer," he said, recalling the dirty tricks of his former advisor Roy Cohn

- During a weekend encounter at the president's Mar-a-Lago property, the president pulled Sessions aside and suggested he "unrecuse" and informed Sessions that former attorneys general Eric Holder and Robert Kennedy had "developed a strategy" to help their presidents

- Comey briefed the "Gang of Eight" congressional leaders about the FBI's investigation into Russian interference

- Notes by McGahn's chief of staff, Annie Donaldson, reflect the tense mood: "POTUS in panic/chaos. . . . Need binders to put in front of POTUS. All things related to Russia."

- Comey publicly revealed the existence of the FBI's investigation into Russia's interference with the 2016 election on March 20, 2017.

- The president asked intelligence community leaders to say publicly he had no connection to Russia.

- He expressed frustration with intelligence leaders that he couldn't fulfill his goals with Russian relations due to the investigation.

- The president asked Comey and other intelligence leaders to "lift the cloud" and publicly proclaim that he had no connection to Russian interference efforts.

He told the FBI director on March 30, 2017, that "the cloud of this Russia business" was making things difficult for him.

The president wanted it to be known that the FBI was not investigating him personally.

- On April 11, 2017, the president called Comey to follow up about telling everyone the president was not personally under investigation.

    Comey said he passed the request to Dana Boente and that there was a proper channel for such a request.

    "I have been very loyal to you, very loyal, we had that thing, you know," the president told Comey.

OBSTRUCTIVE ACT: Following Comey's testimony on March 20, 2017, in which he confirmed that the FBI was investigating links between Russia and the Trump campaign, President Trump "repeatedly reached out to intelligence agency leaders" to discuss the FBI's investigation. While he called for the end of the investigation in some cases, he was more interested in publicly refuting stories linking him and his administration with Russia. According to Mueller, the requests to leaders in the intelligence community "were not interpreted . . . as directives to improperly interfere with the investigation."

NEXUS TO AN OFFICIAL PROCEEDING: At the time of the president's outreach to the intelligence leaders in March and early April 2017, he was aware that the FBI was investigating links between his campaign and Russia and therefore anticipated correlating proceedings.

INTENT: President Trump's contact with intelligence leaders does not establish corrupt intent, but his efforts to stop Sessions's recusal and outreach following Comey's testimony about the FBI investigation is "relevant to understanding what motivated the President's other actions towards the investigation." The president was clearly worried what the implications about Russia would mean for his presidency, saying "the thing with the Russians" was undermining his ability to govern. "The evidence shows that the President was focused on the Russia investigation's implications for his presidency." Trump raised Sessions's recusal on numerous occasions and continued urging Sessions to "unrecuse" himself. The president also expressed to his aides that he wished he had an attorney general "who would protect him." Against the advice of the White House counsel as to the impropriety of direct contact with the FBI, the president reached out to Comey personally and also called on intelligence leaders to make statements that would present him in a positive light. Angered by the Russian probe and negative reports, the president worried the Russia cloud would make it difficult for him to lead the country. "The President complained to advisors that if people thought Russia helped him with the election, it would detract from what he had accomplished."

Frustrated and concerned by the Russia investigation, the president wanted to end the probe at any cost. The president's conduct surrounding Sessions's recusal demonstrated not only his deep-rooted need for loyalty but also his desperate desire to limit and end an investigation that was quickly spinning out of his control.

👎 You're Fired! Events Leading Up to and Surrounding the Termination of FBI Director Comey

EVIDENCE

- During his May 3, 2017, testimony before the Senate Judiciary Committee, James Comey failed to announce that President Trump was not under investigation.
- Days later, the president told close aides he was going to fire Comey.
- He carried out the termination in a May 9, 2017, letter: "Dear Director Comey, While I greatly appreciate your informing me, on three separate occasions, that I am not under investigation concerning the fabricated and politically motivated allegations of a Trump-Russia relationship with respect to the 2016 Presidential Election, please be informed that I, along with both political parties and, most importantly, the American Public, have lost faith in you as the Director of the FBI and you are hereby terminated."

- After drafting the termination letter with senior advisor Stephen Miller, President Trump disclosed his plan to Jeff Sessions and Rod Rosenstein, and neither objected to firing Comey.
- Meeting with a group including White House lawyers, the president suggested that Sessions and Rosenstein put their recommendations about Comey in writing.

    "Put the Russia stuff in the memo," the president said.

    Rosenstein voiced concern with the president's suggestion, saying he in fact didn't consider the Russia investigation a basis for Comey's removal.

    President Trump agreed that Sessions and Rosenstein's memos should serve as the basis for Comey's firing.
- Against advice of counsel, the president asked Miller to draft a new termination letter and insisted that it say Comey had informed him three times he was not under investigation.
- White House lawyers urged that Comey be allowed to resign; the president refused.
- Press Secretary Sean Spicer said the firing was a "DOJ decision."
- President Trump met the following day with Kislyak: "I just fired the head of the FBI. He was crazy, a real nut job. I faced great pressure because of Russia. That's taken off. . . . I'm not under investigation."
- Deputy Press Secretary Sarah Sanders told reporters that the FBI "rank and file" had lost confidence in Comey and that Rosenstein "on his own" came to the president to discuss his concerns with Comey.
- During a May 11, 2017, interview with NBC's Lester Holt, the president admitted that he had decided to fire Comey before meeting with Rosenstein and Sessions. "And in fact, when I decided to just do it, I said to myself—I said, you know, this Russia thing with the president and Russia is a made-up story. It's an excuse by the Democrats for having lost an election that they should've won."
- On May 12, 2017, President Trump tweeted, "James Comey better hope that there are no 'tapes' of our conversations before he starts leaking to the press!"

OBSTRUCTIVE ACT: As Comey had personally briefed the Gang of Eight and publicly testified, his role in the Russia investigation was significant. Nonetheless, firing Comey wouldn't necessarily interfere with or impact the investigation. The FBI could still investigate Trump-world's ties to Russia with or without Comey in office. But the manner in which the president fired the FBI director sent a concerning message: he did it without any warning in a letter delivered to Comey's office by an aide while Comey was visiting his staff in California. Upon Comey's removal, the president banned him from the FBI building and publicly insulted him, calling him a "showboat." "Those actions had the potential to affect a successor director's conduct of the investigation." In his interview with Lester Holt, the president admitted that firing Comey could prolong the investigation. Further evidence of the president's pretextual reasons for removing Comey include his appointment of Andrew McCabe as interim director. McCabe not only worked closely with Comey but also oversaw the FBI's investigation of Hillary Clinton's use of a private email server, the same investigation the president used as a basis for firing Comey.

NEXUS TO AN OFFICIAL PROCEEDING: Comey was fired just weeks after he confirmed that the FBI was investigating links between Trump's campaign and Russia and after he declined to distance Trump from that investigation. And it came as Flynn remained in legal trouble after lying to the FBI. Comey's statements confirmed that the investigation into Trump's campaign, transition, and presidency wasn't going away. At the time of Comey's removal, there were at least two open cases that would inevitably lead to official proceedings: the investigation of the Trump campaign and the investigation of Flynn after meeting with the FBI. Therefore, there was a strong nexus between the president's actions related to Comey's removal and contemplated proceedings.

INTENT: Mueller cites "substantial evidence" that the catalyst for firing Comey was Comey failing to state that the president was not personally under investigation. A sentence in the termination letter about Comey telling President Trump on three occasions he was not under investigation was added at the president's insistence and against Don McGahn's advice. The Special Counsel's Office wasn't buying the president's claim that Comey was fired for poor performance, namely, his handling of the Hillary Clinton email investigation. And Rosenstein's criticism of Comey came after President Trump had already decided to fire the FBI director. Additionally, while the president cited low morale at the FBI, there was no evidence in corroboration. Notably, Mueller considered whether the president's firing of Comey was motivated by the cloud of the Russia investigation over his administration. But the evidence supported the more logical motive, which was the president's desire to "protect himself from an investigation into his campaign" and the fear that an FBI investigation would reveal "facts about the campaign and the President personally that the President could have understood to be crimes or that would give rise to personal and political concerns." Mueller also noted that the president and the White House relied on a fabricated reason for Comey's firing, namely, the letters they requested from Rosenstein and Sessions. Although the evidence doesn't establish whether those motives were personal, political, or both, the president's spin suggests that he "had concerns about providing the real reason for the firing."

The firing of a subordinate is an example of just how challenging it may be to prove whether the act was a legitimate exercise of the president's Article II powers or if it involved corrupt intent. If the president's true basis for removing Comey was dissatisfactory job performance (by a subordinate), then he would be deemed to have used his sweeping presidential powers under the Constitution as opposed to having acted with corrupt intent. However, in light of the totality of the president's acts of obstruction, it's prudent to assume that his removal of Comey was done with corrupt intent and as part of a pattern of conduct aimed at protecting himself and his interests in pending and contemplated proceedings.

👍 Desperate Measures: The President's Efforts
to Remove the Special Counsel

EVIDENCE

- After Sessions recused himself, Mueller was appointed on May 17, 2017.

  President Trump's response: "Oh my God. This is terrible. This is the end of my Presidency. I'm fucked."

  "You were supposed to protect me. . . . This is the worst thing that ever happened to me," the president told Sessions.

- One day after Mueller was appointed, FBI agents delivered a preservation notice to McGahn regarding materials and documents related to the investigation of James Comey's removal.

- Sessions, at President Trump's suggestion, submitted a resignation letter that the president kept without accepting the resignation— something that White House aides considered a "shock collar" that the president could use to manipulate the DOJ.

  The president returned the letter to Sessions on May 30, after he had taken it with him on a trip to Tel Aviv.

- The president asserted to his aides that Mueller had conflicts of interest.

  He claimed Mueller had interviewed for the job of FBI director shortly before being appointed special counsel.

  Mueller once worked for a law firm that represented people close to the president.

  The president claimed Mueller had disputed a decision not to refund his membership fees at a Trump golf course in Virginia after Mueller had moved out of the community.

  The president's advisors pushed back on the bogus conflict of interest claims. Steve Bannon called the so-called conflicts "ridiculous" and in terms of the golf course fees, "petty."

  DOJ ethics officials determined the law firm position did not bar Mueller's service.

- The president asked McGahn to reach out to Rosenstein; McGahn said he would not make the call and that Trump shouldn't either.

  McGahn told the president his efforts to undermine Mueller would be "another fact used to claim obst[ruction] of just[ice]."

  The White House counsel warned the president that his "biggest exposure" wasn't firing Comey; it was his other calls and contacts and his "ask re: Flynn."

- On June 12, 2017, Newsmax Media exec and longtime Trump friend Christopher Ruddy met at the White House with Bannon and Priebus. The aides told Ruddy that the president was considering firing Mueller and that he would do so "without vetting the decision through Administration officials."

  Ruddy floated the possibility of President Trump firing the special counsel in a TV interview based on the so-called conflicts.

  The White House released a statement saying, "While the president has every right to" fire Mueller, "he has no intention to do so."

  President Trump's personal counsel contacted the Special Counsel's Office and highlighted possible conflicts due to Mueller's previous partnership in his law firm and his relationship with Comey.

- On June 15, 2017, the president took to his favorite medium: Twitter. "They made up a phony collusion with the Russians story, found zero proof, so now they go for obstruction of justice on the phony story. Nice."

- Following reports that the president was being investigated for possible obstruction of justice, President Trump called McGahn and "directed him to have the Special Counsel removed because of asserted conflicts of interest." He told McGahn to contact Rosenstein, who would be responsible for removing a special counsel.

  Worried it would spark a "Saturday Night Massacre," McGahn did not comply.

  In fact, the White House counsel saw the president's request as an "inflection point" and prepared to resign. (McGahn declined to share specifics of the president's request with other White House staffers in order not to involve them.)

OBSTRUCTIVE ACT: "The conclusion that the President . . . in fact directed McGahn to call Rosenstein to have the Special Counsel removed" is significant. Despite an abundance of corroborating evidence that supports McGahn's account, the president has vehemently disputed the White House counsel's veracity and accuracy. Specific to the president's orders that "Mueller has to go," he and McGahn spoke twice, and McGahn understood the order similarly both times. Following the request, McGahn decided to quit. President Trump was also raising concerns with the Justice Department about Mueller's so-called conflicts. The president's urgency to take action, on a weekend no less, gave added credibility to McGahn's account. Through his White House aides, the president floated his theory about Mueller's conflicts to Ruddy, and he also reached out to Chris Christie to ask about firing the special counsel. Mueller's take: "This evidence shows that the President was not just seeking an examination of whether conflicts existed but instead was looking to use asserted conflicts as a way to terminate the Special Counsel."

NEXUS TO AN OFFICIAL PROCEEDING: By June 2017 the president was aware that his own conduct was under investigation. In a June 16 tweet he admitted as much: "I am being investigated for firing the FBI Director by the man who told me to fire the FBI Director!" Also grand jury subpoenas were issued in Flynn's inquiry, and reports emerged that the president was being investigated for obstruction of justice—an investigation that could include his firing of Comey, his request for the FBI director to "let Flynn go," and any personal ties he had with Russia. President Trump's actions aimed at the special counsel and the investigation were therefore directly related to multiple contemplated and existing proceedings.

INTENT: Here the president's corrupt intent was blindingly obvious.

The president panicked after Mueller was appointed—"this is the end of my Presidency"—and as reports emerged about investigations into his obstructive behavior, Trump wanted Mueller gone by any means necessary. That included the president seeking to "use his official powers" to direct McGahn to remove the special counsel after Trump had been advised to consult with his personal counsel if he wished to raise conflicts. After reports of the president's orders to McGahn emerged, the president denied it and even tried to get McGahn to refute the truth, showing that the president was aware that his request was improper. Trump's assertion that Mueller had conflicts of interest was a desperate ploy in self-preservation, pure fugazi. His repeated demands to fire the special counsel together with floating the hoax that Mueller's appointment posed conflicts of interest point to one conclusion: that Trump acted with corrupt intent in his endeavor to fire the special counsel, a subordinate of the Justice Department. His conduct was certainly far from related to the execution of a president's official duties, and there was no benign alternative explanation for the president's conduct aimed at removing the special counsel. In sheer desperation to end the investigation into his campaign and himself, the president went to any lengths and abused his power in an effort to remove Mueller.

Rerouting the Witch Hunt: The President's Efforts to Curtail the Special Counsel Investigation

EVIDENCE

- Days after he directed McGahn to remove Mueller, the president took another approach.
- He enlisted his former campaign manager Corey Lewandowski to serve as his messenger and dictated a message for Lewandowski to give to Sessions.

  The president wanted Sessions to announce, in part, "I know that I recused myself from certain things having to do with specific areas. But our POTUS . . . is being treated very unfairly.

He shouldn't have a Special Prosecutor/Counsel b/c he hasn't done anything wrong . . . except he ran the greatest campaign in American history."

The message also included Sessions stating he would meet with Mueller to limit the scope of the investigation to future election interference.

Lewandowski called Sessions to arrange a meeting, but the attorney general had to cancel.

Soon after, Lewandowski left Washington, but he kept the note in a safe at his home.

- Lewandowski met with the president again a month later, and the president repeated the request to have Sessions limit the scope of the investigation.
- Lewandowski never delivered the message.
- President Trump then trashed Sessions in a *New York Times* interview, saying the recusal was "very unfair. . . . If he would have recused himself before the job, I would have said, 'Thanks, Jeff, but I can't, you know, I'm not going to take you.'"
- The president again pushed for Sessions's resignation after it was reported that Sessions had discussed campaign-related issues with the Russian ambassador, Sergey Kislyak.
- President Trump ordered Priebus to demand Sessions's resignation.

    Priebus, feeling uncomfortable about the request, called McGahn for advice, saying it was "all wrong" and that he didn't want to be a part of it.

    McGahn told Priebus not to follow the president's order and suggested they instead consult their personal counsel.
- The president continued to criticize Sessions, so Sessions prepared another resignation letter that for the remainder of the year he kept in his pocket whenever he went to the White House.

OBSTRUCTIVE ACT: President Trump wanted Lewandowski to pass a message to Sessions that read, in part, that the president "shouldn't have a Special Prosecutor/Counsel" and that the attorney general was going to meet with Mueller to explain that the situation was "very unfair" for the president. The president wanted Sessions to disregard his recusal and state that there was no Russian connection with his campaign. And he wanted the attorney general to limit and redirect the special counsel's investigation.

NEXUS TO AN OFFICIAL PROCEEDING: By mid-June 2017 the special counsel was supervising a grand jury investigation of the Trump campaign and investigating the president himself for obstruction of justice. The grand jury was focusing on matters connected to Trump and his family, leaving the president extremely worried about pending and anticipated court proceedings.

INTENT: Trump's effort to have Sessions redirect the special counsel's investigation was specifically intended to prevent further investigations into his campaign and candidacy. Mueller highlights President Trump's pursuit of back channels, including Lewandowski, a private citizen, to deliver the message to Sessions, showing that the president wasn't relying on proper White House protocol because, once again, he knew the request was improper. And by floating talk of Sessions's resignation, the president applied pressure, hoping that with the AG's job on the line, he would comply with the president's demands. The timing of the president's conduct is significant here: his initial request to Lewandowski came just two days after he ordered McGahn to have the special counsel removed. Since we can't get into someone's head, we have to prove corrupt intent through circumstantial evidence, which includes the timing of the acts: the McGahn order to remove the special counsel failed, so within forty-eight hours the president turned to Lewandowski. The evidence is devoid of any facts that would support a noncriminal intent for the president's conduct regarding his desire to terminate the special counsel and in turn the investigation. Clearly, the president acted with corrupt intent.

🖓 The Son Also Rises: The President's Efforts to Prevent Disclosure of Emails about the June 9, 2016, Meeting between Russians and Senior Campaign Officials

EVIDENCE

- Donald Trump Jr. unequivocally welcomed "dirt" on Hillary Clinton.
- In June 2016 the president's oldest son participated in planning for a meeting at Trump Tower that also featured campaign manager Paul Manafort, Trump's son-in-law, Jared Kushner, and Russian attorney Natalya Veselnitskaya.
- Trump Jr. was told in an email that the "Crown prosecutor of Russia" wanted to give the campaign documents and information that would "incriminate Hillary and her dealings with Russia" as a show of Russia's support for Trump.

  "If that's what you say I love it," Trump Jr. responded.
- The meeting also involved Russian adoptions and the Magnitsky Act.
- In 2017 the Senate Select Committee on Intelligence sought information from the Trump campaign about meetings between the campaign and Russia.
- In June 2017 Trump Organization attorneys became aware of the June 2016 meeting and provided the emails to the president's personal counsel.

  Communications Advisor Hope Hicks, along with Kushner and Ivanka Trump, discussed the emails with the president.

  Hicks told the president the emails were "really bad" and the story would be "massive," but Trump said he "did not want details."
- After learning media outlets had begun working on stories about the meeting, Trump directed Hicks not to comment, a tactic the president often considers "the ultimate sin." But eventually he relented and participated in drafting the statement.
- With Trump's input, a draft statement was prepared for Trump Jr. in which he claimed the group "primarily discussed a program

about the adoption of Russian children . . . it was not a campaign issue at the time and there was no follow up."

- As the *New York Times* prepared to publish a story, Trump Jr. posted images of his emails setting up the meeting.
- Press Secretary Sarah Sanders said the president "offered suggestions like any father would do" in drafting the statement for Don Jr.
- The president has long stood by the claim that he had no knowledge of the meeting itself.

OBSTRUCTIVE ACT: On three occasions in late June and early July 2017, President Trump directed Hicks and others not to disclose information about the Trump Tower meeting. After the president rejected his son's draft statement, he dictated a new statement to Hicks, claiming the meeting was about Russian adoption and not information that could be "helpful to the campaign." The acts all involved the president's communications team and were "directed at the press." Mueller therefore didn't find evidence establishing that President Trump took these steps to hinder investigation of the Trump Tower meeting.

NEXUS TO AN OFFICIAL PROCEEDING: Donald Trump Jr.'s emails about the Trump Tower meeting were already obtained in congressional proceedings. Trump Sr. was only trying to prevent their release to the public, not in official proceedings. So while the president engaged in redrafting his son's statement, he was undoubtedly aware of pending and contemplated official proceedings. Nonetheless, his acts appear to have been directed toward preventing or controlling disclosure of the information in the media as opposed to an official proceeding.

INTENT: The evidence was insufficient to conclude that the president acted corruptly in connection with Trump Jr.'s statement regarding the Trump Tower meeting. The Special Counsel's Office and Congress were both in receipt of the emails regarding the meeting. In this instance, it appears that the president's intent was to shield his family from criticism in the media.

᪥ Recusal Refusal: The President's Further Efforts to Have the Attorney General Take Over the Investigation

EVIDENCE

- Jeff Sessions was at home when the president called after the special counsel's appointment in May 2017, asking if he would "unrecuse" himself.

  The president wanted Sessions to direct the DOJ to investigate and prosecute Hillary Clinton, as well as reverse his recusal on "all of it," including the special counsel's Russia investigation.

  The AG listened but did not respond to the president's request and did not follow the directive.

- In early July 2017 the president started asking aide Rob Porter what he thought of Associated Attorney General Rachel Brand to find out if she was "on the team," insinuating that perhaps Brand could replace Sessions as AG.

  Porter didn't follow President Trump's directive because he was "uncomfortable with the task."

  Porter did not contact Brand because he "did not want to be involved in a chain of events associated with an effort to end the investigation or fire the Special Counsel."

- The president talked to Don McGahn about the possibility of working with a nonrecused attorney general.

- In December 2017, after Michael Flynn pleaded guilty to lying about his contacts with Russia, the president again urged Sessions to "unrecuse," telling Sessions he would "be a hero" if he complied.

- "I put in an Attorney General that never took control of the Justice Department, Jeff Sessions," President Trump tweeted on August 23, 2018.

  Sessions pushed back, issuing a statement saying the DOJ's actions "will not be improperly influenced by political considerations."

- One day later, Trump responded: "Jeff, this is GREAT, what everyone wants, so look into all of the corruption on the other side including deleted Emails, Comey lies & leaks, Mueller conflicts, McCabe, Strzok, Page, Ohr, FISA abuse, Christopher Steele & his phony and corrupt Dossier, the Clinton Foundation, illegal surveillance of Trump campaign, Russian collusion by Dems—and so much more. Open up the papers & documents without redaction? Come on, Jeff, you can do it, the country is waiting!"

- On November 7, 2018, the president replaced Sessions as attorney general.

OBSTRUCTIVE ACT: From March 2017 until August 2018, the president repeatedly suggested to Sessions that he should "unrecuse" himself because Trump was interested in guiding the Russia investigation that had ensnared many of his aides as well as prosecuting Clinton.

NEXUS TO AN OFFICIAL PROCEEDING: By June 2017 the special counsel's investigation was circling around the president and his aides. Within months, foreign policy advisor Papadopoulos pleaded guilty and two campaign officials, Manafort and Gates, were indicted. And the president himself was being investigated for obstruction of justice.

INTENT: Following the release of details regarding the June 2016 Trump Tower meeting, the Special Counsel's Office investigation was becoming more and more personal. It now included President Trump's son and son-in-law and himself. The president continued to blame Sessions's decision to recuse himself for the entirety of Mueller's investigation. He seethed to aides about being treated unfairly, suggesting that if somehow the authority of the investigation shifted back to the attorney general, maybe the probe would end. The special counsel infers that President Trump believed "an unrecused Attorney General would play a protective role and could shield the President from the ongoing Russia investigation." The president's unprecedented AG shopping and his numerous attempts to persuade Sessions to unrecuse himself demonstrate corrupt intent to end the investigation against him. His effort to manipulate Sessions reflects an instance of obstruction that's not only indictable but well supported toward a conviction.

🔖 Lawyer, Not Liar: The President Orders McGahn to Deny That the President Tried to Fire the Special Counsel

EVIDENCE

- After news reports emerged about the president's ordering McGahn to have the special counsel fired in June 2017, President Trump, through his personal counsel and two aides, pushed to have McGahn deny the story.

  McGahn refused, standing by the accuracy of the report.

- The president and McGahn later met in the Oval Office, but McGahn again turned down the president's request.

- Privately, the president suggested to staff that McGahn leaked the story to the media "to make himself look good" and called McGahn a "lying bastard."

- President Trump then directed Rob Porter to deliver a message to McGahn, urging him to write a letter denying that he was ordered to fire the special counsel. When McGahn refused, Porter told the lawyer he would be fired if he didn't follow along, which McGahn dismissed, "saying the optics would be terrible if the President followed through with firing him on that basis."

- On February 6, 2018, Chief of Staff John Kelly scheduled a meeting with McGahn and Trump in the Oval Office. "I never said to fire Mueller. I never said 'fire,'" the president said. "This story doesn't look good. You need to correct this. You're the White House counsel."

  President Trump asked McGahn what wording he had used to which McGahn responded: "What you said is, 'Call Rod [Rosenstein], tell Rod that Mueller has conflicts and can't be the Special Counsel."

  "I never said that," the president responded.

  President Trump specifically asked McGahn why he told Mueller's team that Trump wanted Mueller removed, and McGahn replied that their conversations weren't protected by attorney-client privilege.

The president also asked why McGahn took notes of meetings: "Lawyers don't take notes. I never had a lawyer who took notes."

- McGahn responded by saying he was a "real lawyer."
- President Trump: "I've had a lot of great lawyers, like Roy Cohn. He did not take notes."

OBSTRUCTIVE ACT: On the one hand, Mueller raised the possibility that the president truly believed a different version of events than McGahn. On the other hand, "substantial evidence supported McGahn's account that the President had directed him to have the Special Counsel removed." Those details include the timing of the directive, McGahn's reaction, and even the careful wording of President Trump's denials, in which he called the reports "fake news" but didn't offer substantive feedback about what was incorrect. When the president spoke with McGahn in the Oval Office, he focused on one word: "fire." Trump argued he never asked McGahn to fire Mueller. After McGahn declined to walk back the story, the president suggested he might "have to get rid of" the White House counsel if he didn't comply. McGahn again refused. But President Trump continued to ask McGahn to "repudiate facts that McGahn had repeatedly said were accurate."

NEXUS TO AN OFFICIAL PROCEEDING: By January 2018 the special counsel's investigation had returned indictments, and the office had sent the president's counsel a list of topics toward an interview with the president. And by that time, McGahn had already been interviewed by the special counsel. As the obstruction investigation continued, the possibility also remained that he could be interviewed again and asked about the president's calls to fire Mueller.

INTENT: President Trump's repeated efforts to have McGahn walk back his account was a chance for him to "deflect or prevent further scrutiny of the President's conduct towards the investigation." For one, the president requested numerous times that McGahn change his story, even enlisting Porter to apply pressure. Additionally, the president's counsel was so concerned about Trump's meeting with White House counsel that he urged McGahn not to resign. The president even raised the special counsel's investigation in their February 6, 2018, Oval Office meeting when he criticized McGahn for divulging details about his efforts to have Mueller removed. "The President's statements reflect his understanding—and his displeasure—that those events would be part of an obstruction-of-justice inquiry."

The president went to great lengths in his attempts to persuade McGahn to cover up his orders to remove the special counsel. It begs the question: why put so much effort into a cover-up if there's no underlying wrong? As to the president's brazen conduct toward the White House counsel, there is no intent fathomable other than one that is purely corrupt.

👍👎 Silence of the Lambs: The President's Conduct toward Flynn, Manafort, [Redacted]

This section contains heavy redactions that presumably refer to the president's conduct concerning Roger Stone.

EVIDENCE

- President Trump, personally and through his lawyers, used a praise-to-castigation pattern to send messages to his aides who had been charged in the Mueller investigation.
- After Flynn withdrew from a joint defense agreement in late 2017, the president's personal counsel, John Dowd, communicated that Flynn's action would be viewed as "hostility" toward the president.
- Amid Manafort's mounting criminal accusations, Trump consistently spoke about how his former campaign manager was being treated unfairly, and he discussed the possibility that Manafort could receive a pardon.

While offering public praise, the president was privately criticizing Manafort, saying he "never liked" him and didn't think Manafort knew what he was doing on the campaign.

- Manafort told Rick Gates not to plead guilty in early 2018 because Trump's lawyer had said they would "be taken care of."
- Rudy Giuliani, the president's lawyer, also suggested that the Mueller investigation could "get cleaned up with some presidential pardons" when the investigation was over.
- During jury deliberations, the president tweeted about Manafort's case.
- Upon Manafort's guilty verdict in August 2018, the president called him a "good man" and suggested his legal plight was "a very sad thing."

  "Unlike Michael Cohen, he refused to 'break'—make up stories in order to get a 'deal.' Such respect for a brave man!" Trump tweeted.
- In November 2018, after Manafort was accused of having breached his cooperation plea agreement by lying to the special counsel's team, the president suggested in an interview that Manafort was "very brave" because he didn't "flip."

OBSTRUCTIVE ACT: The report concluded emphatically that President Trump's treatment of Manafort "had the potential to influence" his decision on whether to cooperate with the government. Trump and Giuliani's comments suggested a pardon was more likely if Manafort held firm and failed to cooperate, and the president was very clear about not wanting his former campaign manager to flip. Timing is critical when considering Trump's statements and tweets about Manafort. After Manafort's bail was revoked in June 2018, the president called it "very unfair" and suggested it was a "tough sentence." The president continued to make public statements during Manafort's August 2018 trial, even during jury deliberations, calling his case a "hoax" that "continues to stain our country," and later tweeting that Manafort was a "very good person" and the proceedings were "very sad."

And with knowledge that Flynn was under investigation, the president sent private and public messages of comfort and encouragement. But after Flynn entered into a cooperation plea agreement with the special counsel, the president's counsel described Flynn's decision as a reflection of his "hostility" toward the president. This reference may very well have impacted Flynn's decision to cooperate as well as limited the extent of his cooperation. However, because of the protection afforded by the attorney-client privilege, the special counsel couldn't determine whether the president was personally involved or even knew of the communications between his and Flynn's lawyers.

NEXUS TO AN OFFICIAL PROCEEDING: The president's actions toward Flynn and Manafort were directly connected to pending or anticipated legal proceedings. His outreach to Flynn occurred while Flynn was under criminal investigation and it wasn't clear if he would cooperate. His conduct regarding Manafort took things to a whole new level and was "directly connected" to Manafort's official proceedings.

INTENT: The evidence of the president's corrupt intent in his conduct responsive to Flynn was found to be inconclusive. After Flynn pleaded guilty, the president expressed his sympathy for his former national security advisor, saying he felt "very badly." Nevertheless, it was unclear whether the president's messages were meant to prevent Flynn from cooperating with investigators. The evidence regarding the president's response to Manafort, meanwhile, strongly supports one conclusion: that he "intended to encourage Manafort to not cooperate with the government," textbook obstruction of justice involving corrupt intent. Calling Manafort a "brave man" the day after he was sentenced, the president suggested that "flipping . . . almost ought to be outlawed." Privately the president told aides he didn't like Manafort. And since Giuliani floated the idea that the Mueller investigation could get "cleaned up" with presidential pardons, there was a strong inference that the president was dangling a pardon for Manafort, making him less likely to cooperate in hopes of getting a reduced sentence.

Despite the report's extensive fact-finding of the president's obstructive conduct toward Flynn and Manafort, some of the heavy redactions in this section appear to correspond to the president's interactions with Roger Stone. Given the redactions, it's unclear whether Trump has at any time engaged in obstructive acts involving his longtime advisor. Nonetheless, pure speculation would dictate that Stone fits the profile of someone the president would rely on for tricks and cover-ups in conjunction with an open investigation and someone who therefore is deserving of a pardon.

👎 Damn That Flippin' Fixer: The President's Conduct Involving Michael Cohen

"The President's conduct involving Michael Cohen spans the full period of our investigation."

EVIDENCE

- In terms of the Trump Tower Moscow project, which was being pursued at least until June 2016, it was important for candidate Trump to distance himself from any business ties he had with Russia.
- Cohen felt the need to adhere to the "party line" and match the president's account, leading him in 2017 to consult extensively with Trump's counsel, Jay Sekulow, before submitting false statements to Congress and testifying before the Senate Intelligence Committee.

    According to Cohen, Sekulow advised him to keep his statement "short and tight" and not to worry about including too much.
- After it emerged in 2018 that Cohen had arranged a $130,000 payment to prevent Stormy Daniels from publicly disclosing her alleged 2006 tryst with Trump, Cohen released a responsive statement claiming he had used his own money to pay Daniels and that "neither the Trump Organization nor the Trump campaign was a party to the transaction . . . and neither reimbursed me for the payment, either directly or indirectly."

    In fact, the Trump Organization and campaign were a party to the transaction, and Cohen was reimbursed by the company.
- The day after Cohen's statement, he received a text message from President Trump's personal counsel: "Client says thanks for what you do."

- After Cohen's homes and office were raided in April 2018, the president claimed that Cohen wouldn't "flip," privately passed messages of support, and called his longtime fixer a "good man."
- Cohen also spoke with Sekulow about pardons, saying he had been a "loyal lawyer and servant" and that he "wanted to know what was in it for him."
- According to Cohen, Sekulow told him to "stay on message." He called the Mueller investigation a witch hunt "and said that everything else would be fine."
- Cohen believed that as long as he stayed on message, he would be protected by the president, either through a pardon or the investigation being shut down.
- The president's conduct toward Cohen took a drastic turn when Cohen agreed to plead guilty in the Southern District of New York.
- Trump was also furious after learning Cohen recorded him talking about a hush-money payment. He called Cohen a "weak person" and claimed, "I decided not to do" the Moscow project.
- Following Cohen's sentencing, the president tweeted that he "never directed" him to "break the law . . . those charges were just agreed to by him in order to embarrass the president and get a much reduced prison sentence."
- He also called Cohen a "rat" and suggested Cohen's family members had committed crimes.

OBSTRUCTIVE ACT: The special counsel highlighted two issues involving the president's conduct toward Cohen: whether Trump or others aided in Cohen's false statements to Congress, and whether the president took actions that would have the tendency to prevent Cohen from providing truthful information to the government. While there was ample support for the president's knowledge that Cohen provided false testimony, the evidence did not establish that the president had direct input on Cohen's false statements to Congress. Cohen recalled telling Trump that he would "stay on message," but they didn't explicitly discuss the contents of Cohen's testimony about the Trump Tower Moscow project. Instead, Cohen dealt with the president's legal team, including numerous communications with Sekulow, who advised him to avoid details in his statement.

The president's praise-to-castigation pattern was in full effect. First, he urged Cohen not to "flip." After his lawyer spoke to Rudy Giuliani, he told Cohen that he had "friends in high places." Most notably, the president himself told Cohen to "stay strong" and "hang in there." Additionally, Cohen and Sekulow discussed the possibility of a pardon. But as soon as Cohen began meeting with authorities and negotiating a plea agreement, he became the target of attacks and condemnation by the president, who bluntly labeled him a "rat."

NEXUS TO AN OFFICIAL PROCEEDING: The president's support-to-condemnation pattern of conduct toward Cohen occurred as the Special Counsel's Office, Congress, and the U.S. Attorney's Office for the Southern District of New York were investigating Cohen. There was no question that there was a direct correlation between the president's conduct and the pending proceedings involving Cohen.

INTENT: The evidence made it blatantly clear that the president sought to discourage Cohen from cooperating in the pending proceedings that all inevitably involved the president's own conduct. Given his close proximity and relationship with Cohen, the president was undoubtedly concerned that his former fixer might not only share unsavory details about the president, his family, and his companies that could be humiliating but also provide explosive evidence of criminal conduct.

First, Cohen knew the truth about the Trump Tower Moscow discussions: they were extensive and continued into the 2016 presidential primary season as then-candidate Trump was vehemently claiming that he had "no business" in Russia. Based on his direct knowledge of the progress of the Trump Tower Moscow project, the president knew that Cohen was lying to Congress in his opening statement. But instead of highlighting or correcting the substantive inconsistencies and misrepresentations, Sekulow told Cohen that the president "was pleased with what Cohen had said about Trump Tower Moscow." Let's not forget that Cohen's guilty plea for false statements was taken upon an admission that he and Trump had multiple conversations about the project through at least June 2016 and that those talks included plans for a possible trip to Russia "because the project had the potential to be so lucrative."

Second, the president's statements following Cohen's guilty plea demonstrate his grave concerns about what Cohen may have divulged to prosecutors about the Trump Tower Moscow project. At the time the president submitted written answers to the special counsel's questions, Cohen was still cooperating with the Mueller team and hadn't pleaded guilty to making false statements. It therefore wasn't publicly known what, if any, information Cohen might have revealed about the Trump Tower Moscow project. In his written answers to the special counsel, the president did not offer any concrete details about the project, repeatedly citing a lack of recollection. But as soon as Cohen pleaded guilty, the president claimed on Twitter that he himself had decided to abandon the project, a detail that was not in his written answers.

And subsequently the president declined to provide answers to the special counsel's follow-up questions about this discrepancy. The president's conflicting statements about the project were further evidence of his deep concern about the potentially devastating information that Cohen could offer as a witness.

Third, the findings were clear that the president was worried that his former fixer would offer information on topics other than the Moscow project and that Cohen could potentially provide what the president considered false testimony against him in hopes of getting a reduced sentence. The president suggested as much in a November 29, 2018, statement to the media: "He's a weak person . . . what he's trying to do is get a reduced sentence. So he's lying about a project that everybody knew about."

Fourth, the president's statements insinuating that Cohen's father-in-law and wife had committed crimes were an underhanded retaliatory "mob" measure meant to silence Cohen and potentially others who might cooperate against Trump. The timing of those statements, made before Cohen was sentenced and again before he was scheduled to testify before Congress, reflect the president's intent to discourage Cohen from saying anything remotely negative about him. In sum, the special counsel unveiled sufficient facts to support the president's deep concern about matters within Cohen's knowledge that could be damaging to the president, both personally and politically. Against the backdrop of his praise-to-castigation pattern of conduct aimed at Cohen, the president's documented concern supports his corrupt intent to interfere with Cohen's cooperation in the investigation.

The Prosecutor Who Couldn't

Despite having detailed and analyzed an abundance of incriminating evidence against the president, Mueller did not make a "traditional prosecutorial judgment" because he could not. On the very first page of volume 2 of the report, the special counsel unequivocally established the basis for avoiding a determination regarding the president's culpability and indictability. First, he was clear about his adherence to the guidance of the Justice Department's Office of Legal Counsel, which prohibits the indictment or criminal prosecution of a sitting president: "would impermissibly undermine the capacity of the executive branch to perform its constitutionally assigned functions" in violation of "the constitutional separation of powers." He further specified that bringing charges against a sitting president could "preempt constitutional processes" for addressing presidential misconduct. Second, even without an indictment, Mueller found it was also prohibited and unfair to accuse a sitting president of crimes, since he wouldn't be able to defend himself in a court of law:

> If we had confidence after a thorough investigation of the facts that the President clearly did not commit obstruction of justice, we would so state. Based on the facts and the applicable legal standards,

however, we are unable to reach that judgment. Accordingly, while this report does not conclude that the President committed a crime, it also does not *exonerate* him.

In other words, while the special counsel could not recommend indictment or accuse the president of crimes, he most certainly could not and did not clear Trump of crimes.

As a result, the report reads like a prosecution memorandum leading up to a conclusion to recommend indictment but then failing to do so. The special counsel lays out the incriminating facts in painstaking detail and engages in lengthy legal analysis, including why these acts are criminal and why any legal counterarguments are mere hand-waving.

But then, at the denouement, when the conclusion should have read "for these reasons we recommend an indictment," the report radically changes its tune.

Any other American under the same circumstances would be facing a multicount indictment for obstruction of justice under federal law. Simply put, if the second volume of the Mueller report detailed the same evidence and analysis of conduct by Mr. Donald J. Trump and not President Donald J. Trump, it would be an indictment of numerous counts of obstruction of justice replete with overt acts. Perhaps the most surprising conclusion of the special counsel's report is that it "does not exonerate" the president. Prosecutors are in the business of investigation and prosecution toward conviction. Not exoneration. For the past two decades, on behalf of clients charged with similar crimes, exoneration has been *my* daily goal.

Viewing the totality of the special counsel's obstruction of justice investigation and analysis, coupled with the finding that the report is not exonerating the president, can only mean one thing: there *is* in fact sufficient evidence to charge the president with obstruction of justice, and were it not for the protection afforded under DOJ guidance, he would have been indicted.

Your Move, Congress

All eyes were on the special counsel's report for a definite determination not just about Russia's interference in the 2016 election but also the president's criminal liability for obstructive acts. Without a prosecutorial decision regarding indictment, and no determination on criminal liability, the Mueller Report was the first step in a fact-finding quest, leaving it to the constitutional process to hold a sitting president accountable for his crimes. While the special counsel sidestepped a determination regarding the president's culpability and indictment, the report contains many facts that are devastating to the president, the presidency, and to our democracy.

Ahead of the report's release, President Trump's carefully selected attorney general, William Barr, carried out interference efforts on behalf of his boss. Barr's March 24, 2019, purported summary of the Mueller Report grossly mischaracterized Mueller's findings. Barr took it upon himself to exonerate the president, claiming he found "no actions" that constituted obstruction of justice. Barr falsely claimed that Mueller's determination was made without regard to "the constitutional considerations that surround the indictment and criminal prosecution of a sitting president." The attorney general's assertion stands in stark contrast to the truth: that Mueller did not reach a conclusion about Trump's possible criminality, as stated in his written and spoken words. He did not reach such a conclusion because he could not do so, not because he exonerated the president of crimes and certainly not because of insufficient evidence of the president's criminality.

The AG's deliberate misrepresentation of the report provided the president with an ill-gotten victory lap: Trump claimed "exoneration" when Mueller's report expressly stated that he was in fact "not exonerated." The bogus claims of "exoneration" soon metastasized into the president's baseless attacks on Mueller for being "corrupt" and "biased" as well as calls to Barr to investigate the origins of the investigation into Russian interference with the 2016 election. The president even went so far as to suggest, with no evidence whatsoever, that FBI officials including James Comey and Andrew McCabe were guilty of treason, a crime punishable by death. (Of course, they were not; there was no evidence to support the commission of treason by anyone involved in the investigation.)

On May 29, 2019, after two years of quiet, methodical progress and more than a month after his report was released, Mueller finally broke his silence in a ten-minute address from his backyard, the Justice Department headquarters in Washington DC. Mueller chose his words cautiously, standing by the findings of his report and stating he would not testify voluntarily. He confirmed his written words and stated he wouldn't add to them. Although Mueller's remarks may have been yet another disappointment for all who sought closure and clarity, his message was powerful. Mueller's spoken words tore apart the cloud of criticism and gross mischaracterizations that have surrounded his investigation and findings:

- On claims that the investigation was a "witch hunt" and a "hoax": "The matters we investigated were of paramount importance. . . . When a subject of an investigation obstructs that investigation or lies to investigators, it strikes at the core of the government's effort to find the truth and hold wrongdoers accountable."
- On claims that the president was exonerated of any wrongdoing: "If we had had confidence that the president clearly did not commit a crime, we would have said so. We did not, however, make a determination as to whether the president did commit a crime."
- On Congress's role: "First, the opinion explicitly permits the investigation of a sitting President because it is important to preserve evidence while memories are fresh and documents available. . . . And second, the opinion says that the Constitution requires a process other than the criminal justice system to formally accuse a sitting President of wrongdoing."

- On the bottom line: "There were multiple, systematic efforts to interfere in our election. And that allegation deserves the attention of every American."

As expected, the president responded to Mueller's remarks with yet another bogus assertion of exoneration and innocence: "Nothing changes from the Mueller Report. There was insufficient evidence and therefore, in our Country, a person is innocent. The case is closed. Thank you!" In fact, there *was* more than sufficient evidence, the president *was not* exonerated or found innocent, and the case against the president is certainly *not* closed until he is held accountable for the bevy of crimes he committed.

Though addressing the nation at large, Mueller's remarks were especially significant for 535 people: a call for Congress to act on the fruits of his investigation by proceeding with an impeachment inquiry into the president's wrongdoings. Your move, Congress.

CHAPTER 9

PRESIDENTIAL PRECEDENT

A CALL TO ACTION

★ ★ ★ ★ ★

"The Russian government interfered in the 2016 presidential election in sweeping and systematic fashion." The special counsel's report makes it clear that America was the target of an egregious and jarring attack by foreign military units. While not directly linked to arranging those attacks, the president and members of his campaign welcomed Russia's election interference, cheering as a foreign threat assaulted our democratic process, namely, the 2016 election. If the attack had been a terrorist bombing in lieu of a hacking, perhaps the magnitude would be more palpable for Americans.

Experts confirm that our elections remain vulnerable to attacks and that we must be ever more vigilant about the cyberspace activity of foreign and domestic actors. Americans ought to be disturbed and concerned by the lack of clarity and commitment to deter future interference in our elections. While I leave it to the counterintelligence community to safeguard our cybersecurity against future attacks, I find it baffling that Donald Trump, Russia's preferred candidate and the nation's chief executive, is not interested in Mueller's astonishing revelations about election interference. Aside from Trump's outrageous indifference, his multitude of crimes and abuses of power are the most troubling episodes for which he must be held accountable.

The president's conduct is both unprecedented and unpresidential. But most significantly, it is criminal and unconstitutional. As the indictment of a sitting president is prohibited by the Justice Department's

Office of Legal Counsel opinion, the Mueller Report suggested two alternatives: (1) impeachment during his term in office, the "constitutional process," and (2) indictment after serving his term ("while the OLC opinion concludes that a sitting president may not be prosecuted, it recognizes that a president does not have immunity after he leaves office"). In other words, the president could be impeached (and removed by Congress) and the president *may* be indicted once removed or after serving his term, whichever occurs first. Notably presidential immunity is not a perpetual shield against prosecution and justice, and while the statute of limitations is tolled during a president's term, he can be indicted as soon as he leaves the gates of the White House.

President Trump's criminal exposure is most definitely not limited to his blatant obstruction of justice unveiled by the special counsel. He remains an unindicted coconspirator, "Individual-1" in the SDNY case against Michael Cohen for illegal campaign contributions. Moreover, preceding and unrelated to his time in office, Trump and his businesses are the subject of numerous other federal criminal investigations, including the following:

- Trump inaugural committee spending and donations—Southern District of New York
- Investigation into additional matters involving Michael Cohen—Southern District of New York
- Allegations of potential inflated insurance claims—Southern District of New York
- Foreign lobbying violations by Manafort-recruited firms—Southern District of New York
- Unlawful donations by Trump's inaugural committee—Eastern District of New York
- Investigation into GOP donor Li "Cindy" Yang, former massage parlor owner accused of selling access to President Trump—District of Columbia

The bevy of criminal investigations involving Donald J. Trump and his businesses shouldn't be as much a concern to the nation as his criminal conduct during his campaign and while in the Oval Office: campaign finance violations as a candidate followed by brazen acts of obstruction in an investigation into interference with our election and his own conduct.

Accusations of campaign finance violations aren't uncommon. Former Democratic presidential candidate John Edwards was indicted of campaign finance fraud because he used donor gifts to support his mistress, but he wasn't found guilty after it emerged he was trying to hide the affair from his wife, not from voters. And in a civil accusation for campaign finance law violations, Barack Obama's 2008 campaign was fined $375,000 due to missing forty-eight-hour notices. What *is* unprecedented is President Trump's brazen attempts to obstruct an investigation into his own conduct related to the Russia probe, often nefariously abusing his power in connection with orders related to his subordinates.

The president must be held accountable for his crimes, irrespective of venue and process. The federal criminal code is not the only arbiter of a president's criminality. The Constitution can and should be relied on to determine a sitting president's fitness for office. For Trump, accountability could take the following forms:

- Impeachment proceedings and no removal from office, or
- Impeachment proceedings followed by removal from office, and
- Indictment following removal from office; or at the very least,
- Indictment at the end of his presidential term

Nonaccountability is not an option.

The special counsel deferred to Congress to initiate an impeachment inquiry in response to his twenty-two-month investigation. While Mueller didn't mention the I-word in his report, the idea was clearly addressed: "Congress has authority to prohibit a President's corrupt use of his authority in order to protect the integrity of the administration of justice." That authority is in place because the framers of the Constitution contemplated concerns regarding the office of the presidency. Impeachment is the constitutional mechanism by which Congress can hold a president accountable if he fails to execute the laws faithfully or engages in an abuse of power.

There is overwhelming evidence warranting President Trump's impeachment and removal. But the practicality of that proposition is dependent on politics and a highly divided Congress. A coequal branch of government, Congress has the constitutional duty to uphold the law of the land and to conduct oversight of the executive branch. But while political considerations and the likelihood of removal should not be part of the determination to impeach a sitting president, they are.

Article I, Section 2 of the Constitution grants the House of Representatives the power of impeachment, the equivalent of an indictment and formal charges brought by a prosecutor. Article I, Section 3 gives the Senate the sole power to try impeachments, the equivalent of a trial in a court of law. Article II, Section 4 provides: "The President, Vice President and all civil officers of the United States *shall* be removed from office on impeachment for, and conviction of, treason, bribery, or *other high crimes and misdemeanors*."

To ensure Congress doesn't flippantly initiate impeachment proceedings simply because they disagree with a president's policies, impeachment is purposefully an arduous political process. Impeachment of a sitting president requires 218 House votes and 67 Senate votes to remove a sitting president, a two-thirds majority. The proceedings are initiated by the House Judiciary Committee and involve investigations and hearings that could extend over weeks and months.

When most Americans discuss impeachment, they assume that it automatically triggers removal. It does not. Another disappointing truth about impeachment: no sitting U.S. president has *ever* been involuntarily removed from office, and impeachment has only been seriously considered three times in the nation's history. In two of those cases, Andrew Johnson in 1868 and Bill Clinton in 1998–99, the House of Representatives voted to initiate impeachment proceedings, but the Senate, after hearings, fell short of reaching the votes necessary for impeachment. In the third instance, Richard Nixon resigned from office in 1974 before the full House could vote. The bottom line: based on precedent, the chances of removing a sitting president are slim to none. Unfit for office, the impeachment *and removal* of Donald J. Trump would be a necessary but unlikely consequence of his criminal conduct. But the fact that the president may not ultimately be removed from office doesn't make him any less impeachable. And it certainly doesn't change the fact that he is indictable.

The operative legal standard for impeachment of a sitting president is "treason, bribery, or other high crimes and misdemeanors." But what are "high crimes and misdemeanors"? Congress has never passed laws that define what constitutes an impeachable offense. In other words, there is no enumerated list of "high crimes and misdemeanors," a term the framers of the Constitution used to describe a violation of public trust.

There's no way for Congress to imagine and criminalize every possible abuse of power by a president. For that very reason, impeachment is not reserved for "offenses against the United States," language used in the pardon power, but rather for a broader class of "high crimes and misdemeanors." Among the offenses that do constitute "high crimes and misdemeanors" is abuse of authority, which includes obstruction of justice. Many of President Trump's obstructive acts establish a pattern of blatant abuse of power, including

- Dangling pardons to his aides and advisers for their refusal to cooperate
- Directing McGahn to have the special counsel removed because of asserted conflicts of interest
- Enlisting Lewandowski to seek Sessions's unrecusal and refocus on limiting the scope of the investigation
- Seeking Comey's termination of investigation into Flynn and his subsequent firing
- Calling for unwarranted investigations of his rivals

Most notably, the president's power to execute the laws does not give him unfettered authority to stop investigations into his own conduct. He must act in the public's interest, not his own. President Trump abused his power in the most jarring of ways.

As a federal white-collar criminal defense attorney, I respect Mueller's basis for sidestepping a determination regarding the president's culpability and indictability. The Office of Legal Counsel's guidance is a well-established constitutional prohibition, not an arbitrary opinion. But given that laws and regulations must evolve to address unprecedented events and conduct, this may be a call for the Department of Justice to reassess and limit the application of its opinion finding. Instead of a blanket prohibition against indicting a sitting president, no matter what, perhaps the answer is an amendment that provides an exception for indicting a sitting president whose criminal acts were directly related to his candidacy and election. Maybe in at least those instances, the DOJ's Office of Legal Counsel guidance *should* allow indictment of a sitting president.

Despite his belief to the contrary, President Trump is not above the law. Nonetheless, he's indictable but can't be indicted. He's impeachable and removable, but it's an unlikely remedy because of political process. So is he truly *not* above the law?

Every day I fight for justice and endeavor to uphold the constitutional protections afforded to my clients. More than anyone, I value the guarantee that no man is above the law. One day when no longer president, Donald J. Trump *will* be indicted for all of his criminal wrongdoings. But each day that passes without accountability for the president is a day too late. Like many Americans, I feel frustrated by the idea that constitutional prohibitions to the application of federal law and the political hindrance to impeachment are shaping a precedent that just maybe the president is above the law after all. I choose to believe in our laws and our Constitution, and so should you.

No man is above the law, not even the president.

SOURCES

GEORGE D. PAPADOPOULOS

Bever, Lindsey. "Who Is George Papadopoulos, the Trump Adviser Who Pleaded Guilty to Lying to Federal Investigators?" *Washington Post,* October 30, 2017. www.washingtonpost.com/news/politics/wp/2017/10/30/who-is-george -papadopoulos-the-trump-adviser-who-pleaded-guilty-to-lying-to-federal -agents/?utm_term=.4837ad95a9a1.

CNN. Transcript of "The Mysterious Case of George Papadopoulos; George Papadopoulos Ignited the Russia Conspiracy Investigation." September 7, 2018. http://edition.cnn.com/TRANSCRIPTS/1809/07/csr.01.html.

Dreisbach, Tom, and Kelly McEvers. "Former Trump Campaign Adviser Was More than a Coffee Boy, Fiancée Says." *National Public Radio,* February 12, 2018. www.npr.org/2018/02/12/584855759/former-trump-campaign-adviser-was -more-than-a-coffee-boy-fiancee-says.

Edwards, Haley Sweetland. "The Short, Happy Political Career of George Papadopoulos." *Time,* October 31, 2017. http://time.com/5002832/george -papadopoulos-guilty-plea-indictment/.

Hackney, Deanna. "George Papadopoulos Released from Prison." CNN, December 7, 2018. www.cnn.com/2018/12/07/politics/george-papadopoulos-prison/index .html.

Hamburger, Tom, Carol D. Leonnig, and Rosalind S. Helderman. "Trump Campaign Emails Show Aide's Repeated Efforts to Set Up Russia Meetings." *Washington Post,* August 14, 2017. www.washingtonpost.com/politics/trump-campaign -emails-show-aides-repeated-efforts-to-set-up-russia-meetings/2017/08 /14/54d08da6-7dc2-11e7-83c7-5bd5460f0d7e_story.html?utm_term= .49653334d6a6.

Hsu, Spencer S., and Rosalind S. Helderman. "Former Trump Adviser George Papadopoulos Sentenced to 14 Days in Plea Deal with Mueller Probe." *Washington Post,* September 1, 2018. www.washingtonpost.com/local/public -safety/former-trump-adviser-george-papadopoulos-sentenced-to-14-days

-in-plea-deal-with-mueller-probe/2018/09/07/bef367a2-b210-11e8-aed9
-001309990777_story.html?utm_term=.18cbe32ca992.

———. "Former Trump Adviser Papadopoulos Asks Judge to Spare Him Jail Time."
Washington Post, September 1, 2018. www.washingtonpost.com/politics/former
-trump-adviser-the-first-charged-in-mueller-probe-asks-judge-to-spare-him
-jail-time/2018/09/01/4bb27c3c-abc7-11e8-a8d7-0f63ab8b1370_story.html
?utm_term=.4bc99c80e042.

Jalonick, Mary Clare. "Five People in Donald Trump's Political Orbit Who Have
Pleaded Guilty." *Wisconsin State Journal*, September 21, 2018. madison
.com/news/nation/government-and-politics/five-people-in-donald-trump-s
-political-orbit-who-have/collection_7fc45ca6-0e0d-5be1-931b-27b4af03a8ca
.html#2.

Johnson, Alex. "Who Is George Papadopoulos? Energy Expert and Junior Trump
Staffer Sought to Be Russia Power Broker." NBC News, October 30, 2017. www
.nbcnews.com/news/us-news/who-george-papadopoulos-energy-expert-junior
-trump-staffer-sought-be-n815826.

LaFraniere, Sharon, Mark Mazzetti, and Matt Apuzzo. "How the Russia Inquiry
Began: A Campaign Aide, Drinks, and Talk of Political Dirt." *New York Times*,
December 30, 2017. www.nytimes.com/2017/12/30/us/politics/how-fbi-russia
-investigation-began-george-papadopoulos.html.

Landers, Elizabeth. "Trump Dismisses Papadopoulos as 'Low-Level Volunteer' but
Once Touted Him." CNN, October 31, 2017. www.cnn.com/2017/10/31/politics
/donald-trump-george-papadopoulos/index.html.

Meisner, Jason, and Patrick M. O'Connell. "Week after Bombshell, George
Papadopoulos Largely Remains a Mystery Man." *Chicago Tribune*, November
7, 2017. www.chicagotribune.com/news/local/breaking/ct-met-george
-papadopoulos-russian-investigation-20171102-story.html.

Paton, Callum. "Stephen Miller in Regular Contact with George Papadopoulos,
as Were Other Top Trump Officials." *Newsweek*, November 11, 2017. www
.newsweek.com/stephen-miller-regular-contact-george-papadopoulos-were
-other-top-trump-708802.

Sanders, Linley. "George Papadopoulos Lied on His Resume to Get Trump
Campaign Foreign Policy Job, Former Employer Says." *Newsweek*, November 1,
2017. www.newsweek.com/george-papadopoulos-lied-his-resume-698409.

Tanfani, Joseph, Noah Bierman, and Brian Bennett. "Special Counsel Named to
Head Russia Investigation; White House Caught by Surprise." *Los Angeles
Times*, May 17, 2017. www.latimes.com/politics/washington/la-na-essential
-washington-updates-former-fbi-director-robert-mueller-1495058507
-htmlstory.html.

U.S. Code, 18 U.S.C. § 1001 (GPO). www.gpo.gov/fdsys/pkg/USCODE-2011-title18
/pdf/USCODE-2011-title18-partI-chap47-sec1001.pdf.

U.S. Government. *United States v. George Papadopoulos*. "[Criminal] Information"
(on file).

———. *United States v. George Papadopoulos.* "Plea Agreement" (on file).

———. *United States v. George Papadopoulos.* "Sentencing Memo" (on file).

———. *United States v. George Papadopoulos.* "Statement of the Offense." www
.justice.gov/file/1007346/download.

Vazquez, Meagan. "Ex-Trump Campaign Adviser: Papadopoulos Was Just a 'Coffee
Boy.'" CNN, October 31, 2017. www.cnn.com/2017/10/31/politics/caputo
-papadopoulos-coffee-boy-cnntv/index.html.

Witte, Griff, and Karla Adam. "Is There More than Meets the Eye with the Professor
at the Center of the Trump-Russia Probe? Or Less?" *Washington Post.*
November 4, 2017. www.washingtonpost.com/world/europe/is-there-more-than
-meets-the-eye-with-the-professor-at-the-center-of-the-trump-russia-probe
-or-less/2017/11/03/4e95ec48-c006-11e7-9294-705f80164f6e_story.html
?utm_term=.044b05dbbbda.

LT. GEN. (RET.) MICHAEL FLYNN

Brown, Pamela, Jeremy Herb, Katelyn Polantz, and Kaitlan Collins. "Flynn
Contacted GOP Mueller Critic While Cooperating with Special Counsel." CNN,
May 17, 2019. www.cnn.com/2019/05/17/politics/michael-flynn-mueller-matt
-gaetz/index.html.

CNN. "Michael Flynn Leads 'Lock Her Up' Chant at 2016 RNC." CNN, December 1,
2017. www.youtube.com/watch?v=tx94428MYcc.

House Oversight Committee. May 16, 2017. oversight.house.gov/news/press-releases
/cummings-releases-new-documents-confirming-that-flynn-received-funds
-from.

McCaskill, Nolan D. "5 Times Trump Defended Flynn." *Politico*, December 1, 2017.
www.politico.com/story/2017/12/01/what-trump-has-said-about-michael-flynn
-274454.

Polantz, Katelyn. "Transcript Released of Flynn Voicemail from Trump Lawyer
Showing Possible Attempt to Obstruct." CNN, May 31, 2019. www.cnn.com/2019
/05/31/politics/michael-flynn-john-dowd-voicemail/
index.html.

U.S. Code, 18 U.S.C. § 1001 (GPO). www.gpo.gov/fdsys/pkg/USCODE-2011-title18
/pdf/USCODE-2011-title18-partI-chap47-sec1001.pdf.

U.S. Government. *United States v. Michael T. Flynn.* "Criminal Information"
(on file).

———. *United States v. Michael T. Flynn.* "Defendant's Memorandum in Aid of
Sentencing" (on file).

———. *United States v. Michael T. Flynn.* "Government's Memorandum in Aid of
Sentencing" (on file).

———. *United States v. Michael T. Flynn.* "Plea Agreement" (on file).

———. *United States v. Michael T. Flynn.* "Statement of the Offense" (on file).

———. "Report on the Investigation into Russian Interference in the 2016
Presidential Election" (on file).

RICK GATES

Gates Group International. "Rick Gates, Chairman." web.archive.org/web
/20171103151811/http://gatesgroupintl.com/?page_id=78.

Jacobs, Jennifer. "Kellyanne Conway Takes on Toughest Role Yet: Trump Whisperer."
Chicago Tribune, August 18, 2016. www.chicagotribune.com/nation-world/ct
-kellyanne-conway-trump-campaign-20160818-story.html.

Peoples, Steve, and Jeff Horwitz. "Rick Gates: A Trump Survivor Is Tested by
Mueller Probe." Associated Press, November 2, 2017. www.apnews.com
/8a3454b867634cdb83c435c38c51ba58.

Prokop, Andrew. "Top Mueller Cooperator Rick Gates Continues to Cooperate with
Several Investigators." *Vox*, March 15, 2019. www.vox.com/policy-and-politics
/2019/3/15/18267290/mueller-rick-gates-trump-russia-inauguration.

Smith, Jeremy Silk. "Who's Going to Get Fired over Melania Trump Speech?" *Roll
Call*, July 19, 2016. www.rollcall.com/news/politics/rick-gates-melania-trump
-speech-plagiarism.

U.S. Code, 18 U.S.C. § 371 (GPO). www.govinfo.gov/app/details/USCODE-2011
-title18/USCODE-2011-title18-partI-chap19-sec371.

U.S. Government. *United States v. Paul J. Manafort, Jr., and Richard W. Gates III.*
"Indictment" (on file).

———. *United States v. Paul J. Manafort, Jr.* "Exhibits" (on file).

———. *United States v. Paul J. Manafort, Jr.* "Plea Agreement" (on file).

———. *United States v. Paul J. Manafort, Jr.* "Statement of the Offense" (on file).

———. *United States v. Paul J. Manafort, Jr.* "Superseding Criminal Information"
(on file).

———. *United States v. Richard W. Gates III.* "Plea Agreement" (on file).

———. *United States v. Richard W. Gates III.* "Statement of the Offense" (on file).

———. *United States v. Richard W. Gates III.* "Superseding Criminal Information"
(on file).

———. "Report on the Investigation into Russian Interference in the 2016
Presidential Election" (on file).

Vogel, Kenneth P., and Isaac Arnsdorf. "Trump Campaign Brings in Lobbyists for
Key Posts." *Politico*, April 20, 2016. www.politico.com/story/2016/04/trump
-turns-over-his-campaign-to-lobbyists-222242.

Wertheimer, Fred, and Norman Eisen. "Trump Illegally Asked Russia to Help Him
Win in 2016. He Shouldn't Get Away with It." *USA Today*, January 2, 2019. www
.usatoday.com/story/opinion/2019/01/02/trump-broke-law-russia-clinton
-emails-hold-him-accountable-column/2449564002/.

PAUL MANAFORT

"Biographies of Presidential Personnel Office Staff." Gerald R. Ford Presidential
Library and Museum. www.fordlibrarymuseum.gov/library/guides/findingaid
/ppo_bio.pdf, 20.

C-Span. "President Trump Remarks on Manafort Trial." August 21, 2018. www.c
-span.org/video/?450351-1/president-trump remarks-paul-manafort-verdict.

"Donald Trump's Public Statements." Votesmart.org. votesmart.org/candidate
/public-statements/15723/donald-trump?search=manafort&start=&end=#
.XOvxbuhKiUk.

Foer, Franklin. "Paul Manafort, American Hustler." *Atlantic*. March 2018. www
.theatlantic.com/magazine/archive/2018/03/paul-manafort-american-hustler
/550925/.

"How a Well-Connected Political Firm Pitches a Foreign Nation." *O'Dwyer's PR
Services Report*, January 1990. Retrieved from www.nexis.com.

Keating, Christopher. "Running a Tight, Quiet Ship." *Hartford Courant*, August 15,
1996. Retrieved from www.newspapers.com.

Leukhardt, Bill. "Former New Britain Mayor Paul Manafort Dies." *Hartford Courant*,
January 25, 2013. Retrieved from www.nexis.com.

"Paul John Manafort." In *Who's Who in the South and Southwest*. 23rd ed., 1993–
1994. New Providence NJ: Marquis Who's Who, 1993. Retrieved from www
.nexis.com.

Rainey, James. "Convention Boss Gives GOP a Lift from the Wings." *Los Angeles
Times*, August 15, 1996. Retrieved from www.newspapers.com.

Shapiro, Walter, Margaret Garrard Warner, and Howard Fineman. "Cashing In on
Reagan." *Newsweek*, March 3, 1986. Retrieved from www.nexis.com.

Tucker, Eric. "Trump Tower Meeting Emails 'Really Bad,' Aide Told Trump." April 25,
2019. www.apnews.com/215ffd4a7c25473abd5a0b1781bb947b.

U.S. Code, 18 U.S.C. § 371 (GPO). www.govinfo.gov/app/details/USCODE-2011
-title18/USCODE-2011-title18-partI-chap19-sec371.

U.S. Code, 18 U.S.C. § 1512. www.justice.gov/jm/criminal-resource-manual-1729
-protection-government-processes-tampering-victims-witnesses-or.

U.S. Code, 18 U.S.C. § 1344. www.justice.gov/jm/criminal-resource-manual-826
-applicability-18-usc-1344.

U.S. Code, 18 U.S.C. § 3553. www.law.cornell.edu/uscode/text/18/3553.

U.S. Code, 31 U.S.C. § 5314. www.govinfo.gov/app/details/USCODE-2011-title31
/USCODE-2011-title31-subtitleIV-chap53-subchapII-sec5314.

U.S. Government. *In the Matter of the Search of Hard Drive with Serial Number
WXB1AA006666*. "Application for a Search Warrant" (on file).

——— . "Report on the Investigation into Russian Interference in the 2016
Presidential Election" (on file).

——— . *United States v. Paul J. Manafort, Jr.* "Superseding Criminal Information"
(on file).

——— . *United States v. Paul J. Manafort, Jr.* "Exhibits" (on file).

——— . *United States v. Paul J. Manafort, Jr.* "Plea Agreement" (on file).

——— . *United States v. Paul J. Manafort, Jr.* "Statement of the Offense" (on file).

——— . *United States v. Paul J. Manafort, Jr., and Richard W. Gates III*. "Indictment"
(on file).

Welch, William M. "Former HUD Official Says He Did Nothing Wrong in Advising Bush Campaign." Associated Press, October 24, 1989. Retrieved from www.nexis.com.

Yancey, Matt. "Developer Acquitted in HUD Scandal." January 28, 1993. Retrieved from www.nexis.com.

MICHAEL COHEN

Cohen, Marshall, and Katelyn Polantz. "Federal Court Unseals Michael Cohen Search Warrants, Further Detailing His Russian Ties." CNN, May 22, 2019. www.cnn.com/2019/05/22/politics/michael-cohen-search-warrants/index.html.

Cuomo, Chris, Kara Scannell, and Eli Watkins. "Exclusive: CNN Obtains Secret Trump-Cohen Tape." CNN, July 25, 2018. www.cnn.com/2018/07/24/politics/michael-cohen-donald-trump-tape/index.html.

Falcone, Michael. "Donald Trump's Political 'Pit Bull': Meet Michael Cohen." ABC News, April 16, 2011. abcnews.go.com/Politics/donald-trumps-political-pit-bull-meet-michael-cohen/story?id=13386747.

Fox, Emily Jane. "Michael Cohen Would Take a Bullet for Donald Trump." *Vanity Fair*, September 6, 2017. www.vanityfair.com/news/2017/09/michael-cohen-interview-donald-trump.

GOP.com. "RNC Announces Additions to RNC Finance Leadership Team." (April 3, 2017). https://web.archive.org/web/20170404015057/https://gop.com/rnc-announces-additions-to-rnc-finance-leadership-team/.

Hamburger, Tom, Ellen Nakashima, and Karoun Demirjian. "Cohen Told Lawmakers Trump Attorney Jay Sekulow Encouraged Him to Falsely Claim Moscow Project Ended in January 2016." *Washington Post*. May 20, 2019. www.washingtonpost.com/politics/cohen-told-lawmakers-trump-attorney-jay-sekulow-instructed-him-to-falsely-claim-moscow-project-ended-in-january-2016/2019/05/20/e98c6a5e-7b0f-11e9-8bb7-0fc796cf2ec0_story.html?utm_term=.b05e5d44587f.

"Michael Cohen." Biography.com. www.biography.com/law-figure/michael-cohen.

"Michael Cohen." LinkedIn. www.linkedin.com/in/michaelcohen3.

Stephanopoulos, George. "Exclusive: Michael Cohen Says Family and Country, Not President Trump, Is His 'First Loyalty.'" ABC News, July 2, 2018. abcnews.go.com/Politics/michael-cohen-family-country-president-trump-loyalty/story?id=56304585.

Toobin, Jeffrey. "Michael Cohen's Last Days of Freedom." *New Yorker*, April 29, 2019. www.newyorker.com/magazine/2019/05/06/michael-cohens-last-days-of-freedom.

U.S. Code, 26 U.S.C. § 7201. www.govinfo.gov/app/details/USCODE-2011-title26/USCODE-2011-title26-subtitleF-chap75-subchapA-partI-sec7201.

U.S. Code, 18 U.S.C. § 1014. www.justice.gov/jm/criminal-resource-manual-814-false-statements-18-usc-1014.

U.S. Code, Title 52. www.law.cornell.edu/uscode/text/52.

U.S. Government. "Report on the Investigation into Russian Interference in the 2016 Presidential Election" (on file).

———. *United States v. Michael Cohen*. "Criminal Information" (on file).

———. *United States v. Michael Cohen*. "Plea Agreement" (on file).

———. *United States v. Michael Cohen*. "Sentencing Memorandum" (on file).

U.S. House of Representatives. "Testimony of Michael D. Cohen Committee on Oversight and Reform." *Politico*, February 27, 2019. www.politico.com/f/?id=00000169-2d31-dc75-affd-bfb99a790001.

ROGER STONE

Bump, Philip. "A Timeline of the Roger Stone–WikiLeaks Question." *Washington Post*, October 30, 2018. www.washingtonpost.com/politics/2018/10/30/timeline-roger-stone-wikileaks-question/?utm_term=.6f40fab427e1.

Chuck, Elizabeth. "Trump and Top Strategist Roger Stone Split after Megyn Kelly Remarks." NBC News, August 8, 2015. www.nbcnews.com/politics/2016-election/trumps-megan-kelly-comment-draws-ire-gop-costs-him-top-n406481.

Mangan, Dan, and Kevin Breuninger. "Judge Imposes Full Gag Order on Roger Stone after He Apologizes for 'Stupid' Instagram Crosshair Post." CNBC, February 21, 2019. www.cnbc.com/2019/02/21/roger-stone-will-testify-to-explain-crosshair-instagram-post.html.

"The Rise and Gall of Roger Stone: The Political Strategist, Playing Hardball." *Washington Post*, June 16, 1986. Retrieved from www.nexis.com.

"Roger Jason Stone Jr." *Who's Who in the South and Southwest*. 26th ed., 2014. New Providence NJ: Marquis Who's Who, 2014. Retrieved from www.nexis.com.

Roger Stone on Instagram. www.instagram.com/rogerjstonejr/?hl=en.

Samuelsohn, Darren, Josh Gerstein, and Matthew Choi. "Judge Broadens Gag Order against Roger Stone after Instagram Post." *Politico*, February 21, 2019. www.politico.com/story/2019/02/21/roger-stone-gag-order-1179548.

"Sex Flap Hits GOPer." *New York Daily News*, September 13, 1996. Retrieved from www.nexis.com.

Stone, Roger. "Dear Hillary: DNC Hack Solved, So Now Stop Blaming Russia." *Breitbart*, August 5, 2016. www.breitbart.com/politics/2016/08/05/dear-hillary-dnc-hack-solved-so-now-stop-blaming-russia/.

Toobin, Jeffrey. "The Dirty Trickster." *New Yorker*, May 23, 2008. www.newyorker.com/magazine/2008/06/02/the-dirty-trickster.

United Press International. "Making a Scene." *People*, December 9, 1991. "A few hours later Trump and Maples were seen smiling and holding hands at a wedding reception for Republican consultant Roger Stone and Nydia Bertran. When asked about the state of their relationship, Maples said, 'Great! He allows me to work, but I think he prefers if I didn't.'" Retrieved from www.nexis.com.

U.S. Code, 18 U.S.C. § 1001 (GPO). www.gpo.gov/fdsys/pkg/USCODE-2011-title18 /pdf/USCODE-2011-title18-partI-chap47-sec1001.pdf.

U.S. Code, 18 U.S.C. § 1505. www.justice.gov/jm/criminal-resource-manual-1725 -protection-government-processes-obstruction-pending-proceeding-18.

U.S. Code, 18 U.S.C. § 2. www.law.cornell.edu/uscode/text/18/2.

U.S. Code, 18 U.S.C. § 1512. www.justice.gov/jm/criminal-resource-manual-1729 -protection-government-processes-tampering-victims-witnesses-or.

U.S. Government. "Final Report of the Senate Select Committee on Presidential Campaign Activities." www.maryferrell.org/showDoc.html?docId=144965& search=roger_stone#relPageId=1&tab=page.

——. *United States v. Roger Jason Stone, Jr.* "Indictment" (on file).

——. *United States v. Viktor Borisovich Netyksho, et al.* "Indictment" (on file).

U.S. House of Representatives. "Testimony of Michael D. Cohen Committee on Oversight and Reform." *Politico*, February 27, 2019. www.politico.com/f/?id= 00000169-2d31-dc75-affd-bfb99a790001.

PARDON ME, PARDON WHO?

Beavers, Olivia. "Barr: It Would Be a Crime for President to Pardon Someone in Exchange for Their Silence." *The Hill*, January 15, 2019. thehill.com/homenews /senate/425404-trumps-ag-pick-it-would-be-a-crime-if-a-president-pardoned -individual-in.

Black, Conrad. *Donald Trump: A President Like No Other*. Washington DC: Regnery, 2018.

CBS News. "Transcript: President Trump on *Face the Nation*, February 3, 2019." www .cbsnews.com/news/transcript-president-trump-on-face-the-nation-february-3 -2019/.

Donald Trump on Twitter (August 22, 2018). twitter.com/realdonaldtrump/status /1032256443985084417?lang=en.

Editorial Board. "The President and His Power to Pardon." *New York Times*, May 19, 2019. www.nytimes.com/2019/05/19/opinion/trump-pardon-conrad-black -patrick-nolan.html.

Egan, Lauren, and Dartunorro Clark. "Trump Says He 'Feels Very Badly' about Manafort Convictions, Attacks Mueller." NBC News, August 21, 2018. www .nbcnews.com/politics/politics-news/trump-says-he-feels-very-badly-about -manafort-convictions-attacks-n902696.

Fabian, Jordan. "Trump Mum on Manafort Pardon: 'It's a Very Sad Situation.'" *Hill*, March 13, 2019. thehill.com/homenews/administration/433909-trump-mum -on-manafort-pardon-its-a-very-sad-situation.

Holson, Laura M. "'No One Could Believe It': When Ford Pardoned Nixon Four Decades Ago." *New York Times*, September 8, 2018. www.nytimes.com/2018/09 /08/us/politics/nixon-ford-pardon-watergate.html.

Johnston, David. "Bush Pardons 6 in Iran Affair, Aborting a Weinberger Trial; Prosecutor Assails 'Cover-up.'" *New York Times*. December 25, 1992. archive

.nytimes.com/www.nytimes.com/books/97/06/29/reviews/iran-pardon.html
?mcubz=0.

Kruzel, John. "No, the FBI Did Not Say Michael Flynn Did Not Lie, as Donald
Trump Said." *Politifact*, March 28, 2019. www.politifact.com/truth-o-meter
/statements/2019/mar/28/donald-trump/no-fbi-did-not-say-michael-flynn-did
-not-lie-donal/.

Legal Information Institute. Article II, U.S. Constitution. www.law.cornell.edu
/constitution/articleii.

Liptak, Kevin. "Trump's Pardons Appear Prompted by TV, Friends, and Politics."
CNN, May 21, 2019. www.cnn.com/2019/05/21/politics/donald-trump-pardons
-pattern/index.html.

NDA9. "Trump on Kim Kardashian." C-Span, June 8, 2018. www.c-span.org/video/
?c4743765/trump-kim-kardashian.

Rodrigo, Chris Mills. "Papadopoulos Says His Lawyers Have Asked for a Pardon
from Trump." *Hill*, March 26, 2019. thehill.com/homenews/administration
/435905-papadopoulos-says-his-lawyers-have-formally-asked-trump-for
-pardon.

Rubin, Jennifer. "A Trump-Era Challenge: Separating the Vile from the Merely
Dangerous." *Washington Post*, June 1, 2018. www.washingtonpost.com/blogs
/right-turn/wp/2018/06/01/a-trump-era-challenge-separating-the-vile-from
-the-merely-dangerous/?utm_term=.1f9383c70715.

Sommerfeldt, Chris. "Rudy Giuliani Says Mueller Probe 'Might Get Cleaned Up' with
'Presidential Pardons' in Light of Paul Manafort Going to Jail." *New York Daily
News*, June 15, 2018. www.nydailynews.com/news/politics/ny-news-rudy-muller
-pardons-trump-manafort-20180615-story.html.

U.S. Department of Justice. "Pardons Granted by President Donald Trump." www
.justice.gov/pardon/pardons-granted-president-donald trump.

———. "Pardons Granted by President William J. Clinton." www.justice.gov/pardon
/clinton-pardons.

U.S. Government. "Report on the Investigation into Russian Interference in the 2016
Presidential Election" (on file).

THE MUELLER REPORT

Barr, William. Letter to Congress detailing Robert Mueller's findings in the Russia
Investigation, March 24, 2019. www.documentcloud.org/documents/5779699
-Letter-to-Congress-detailing-Robert-Mueller-s.html.

Barrett, Devlin, and Matt Zapotosky. "Mueller Complained That Barr's Letter
Did Not Capture 'Context' of Trump." *Washington Post*, April 30, 2019. www
.washingtonpost.com/world/national-security/mueller-complained-that-barrs
-letter-did-not-capture-context-of-trump-probe/2019/04/30/d3c8fdb6-6b7b
-11e9-a66d-a82d3f3d96d5_story.html.

Hains, Tim. "Watch: Moment in April 9 Testimony Where AG Bill Barr Is Said
to Have Lied about Mueller Report." *Real Clear Politics*, May 2, 2019. www

.realclearpolitics.com/video/2019/05/02/watch_moment_in_congressional
_testimony_where_ag_bill_barr_is_said_to_have_lied.html.

Isikoff, Michael. "Chinese Hacked Obama, McCain Campaigns, Took Internal
Documents, Officials Say." NBC News, June 10, 2013. http://www.nbcnews
.com/id/52133016/t/chinese-hacked-obama-mccain-campaigns-took-internal
-documents-officials-say/#.XOwrtOhKiUk.

Justia. *United States v. Aguilar, 515 U.S. 595 (1995).* supreme.justia.com/cases/federal
/us/515/593/.

LaFraniere, Sharon, Mark Mazzetti, and Matt Apuzzo. "How the Russia Inquiry
Began: A Campaign Aide, Drinks, and Talk of Political Dirt." *New York Times,*
December 30, 2017. www.nytimes.com/2017/12/30/us/politics/how-fbi-russia
-investigation-began-george-papadopoulos.html.

Polantz, Katelyn. "Transcript Released of Flynn Voicemail from Trump Lawyer
Showing Possible Attempt to Obstruct." CNN, May 31, 2019. www.cnn.com/2019
/05/31/politics/michael-flynn-john-dowd-voicemail/index.html.

"A Sitting President's Amenability to Indictment and Criminal Prosecution."
Department of Justice website, October 16, 2000. www.justice.gov/olc/opinion
/sitting-president%E2%80%99s-amenability-indictment-and-criminal
-prosecution.

U.S. Government. "Report on the Investigation into Russian Interference in the 2016
Presidential Election" (on file).

PRESIDENTIAL PRECEDENT

Associated Press (via Brooklyn College). "The Articles of Impeachment against
Nixon." http://academic.brooklyn.cuny.edu/history/johnson/rnimparticles.htm.

Baker, Peter. "Trump Declares a National Emergency, and Provokes a Constitutional
Clash." *New York Times.* February 15, 2019. www.nytimes.com/2019/02/15/us
/politics/national-emergency-trump.html.

Conway, Michael. "Trump's Impeachment Doesn't Have to Wait. The Founding
Fathers Never Wanted It to Be an Insurmountable Hurdle." NBC News, March
17, 2019. www.nbcnews.com/think/opinion/trump-s-impeachment-doesn-t
-have-wait-founding-fathers-never-ncna984051.

"The Federalist Papers: No. 65." Avalon Project, March 7, 1788. http://avalon.law.yale
.edu/18th_century/fed65.asp.

Feldman, Noah. "The Prosecutors Who Have Declared War on the President."
Bloomberg.com, August 26, 2018. www.bloomberg.com/opinion/articles/2018
-08-26/southern-district-of-new-york-will-tear-into-trump-organization.

Haberman, Maggie. "Obama 2008 Campaign Fined $375,000." *Politico,* January 4,
2013. www.politico.com/story/2013/01/obama-2008-campaign-fined-375000
-085784.

Haberman, Maggie, and Ben Protess. "Trump Inaugural Committee Ordered to
Hand Over Documents to Federal Investigators." *New York Times,* February 4,

2019. www.nytimes.com/2019/02/04/us/politics/trump-inaugural-committee-subpoena.html.

Law, Tara. "Bill Clinton Was Impeached 20 Years Ago. Here's How the Process Actually Works." *Time*, December 18, 2018. http://time.com/5477435/impeachment-clinton/.

National Constitution Center. "Article 1: Legislative Branch." constitutioncenter.org/interactive-constitution/articles/article-i.

Newport, Frank. "Presidential Job Approval: Bill Clinton's High Ratings in the Midst of Crisis, 1998." Gallup, June 4, 1999. news.gallup.com/poll/4609/presidential-job-approval-bill-clintons-high-ratings-midst.aspx.

Niemietz, Brian. "'No Redos for Dems!' Trump Lashes Out on Democrats' Push to Get Robert Mueller to Testify before House Committee." *New York Daily News*, May 5, 2019. www.nydailynews.com/news/national/ny-robert-mueller-congress-house-judicial-commitee-20190505-vkca2xtw35gp7m66ebbgjkxj4e-story.html.

"The Options for Impeaching Trump." *Slate*, April 18, 2017. http://www.slate.com/articles/news_and_politics/trumpcast/2017/04/corruption_abuse_of_power_and_undermining_the_rule_of_law_the_case_for_impeaching.html.

Roland, John. "Meaning of High Crimes and Misdemeanors." *Constitution Society*, January 16, 1999. www.constitution.org/cmt/high_crimes.htm.

Scannell, Kara. "Prosecutors Examining Tens of Thousands of Trump Inauguration Documents." CNN, May 20, 2019. www.cnn.com/2019/05/20/politics/trump-inaugural-prosecutors-new-york/index.html.

Stracqualursi, Veronica. "Top Democrat: DOJ 'Needs to Re-examine' Guidance That a Sitting President Shouldn't Be Indicted." CNN, December 13, 2018. www.cnn.com/2018/12/12/politics/adam-schiff-doj-guidance-president-indictment-cnntv/index.html.

U.S. Government. "Report on the Investigation into Russian Interference in the 2016 Presidential Election" (on file).

U.S. Senate. "The Impeachment of Andrew Johnson (1868) President of the United States." www.senate.gov/artandhistory/history/common/briefing/Impeachment_Johnson.htm.

Vogel, Kenneth P. "Firms Recruited by Paul Manafort Are Investigated over Foreign Payments." *New York Times*, February 5, 2019. www.nytimes.com/2019/02/05/us/politics/paul-manafort-news-ukraine.html.

Weaver, Jay, Sarah Blaskey, Caitlin Ostroff, and Nicholas Nehamas. "Federal Prosecutors Demand Cindy Yang Records from Mar-a-Lago, Trump Campaign." *Miami Herald*, May 29, 2019. www.miamiherald.com/news/politics-government/article230946518.html.

Zeldin, Michael. "Abuse of Power, Not Obstruction, Should Keep Trump's Legal Team on Edge." CNN, June 15, 2017. www.cnn.com/2017/06/15/opinions/trump-obstruction-abuse-of-power-opinion-zeldin/index.html.